# The Rise of
# Legal Services Outsourcing

# The Rise of Legal Services Outsourcing

## Risk and Opportunity

**Professor Mary Lacity**
University of Missouri-St. Louis,
Visiting Professor,
The London School of Economics and
Political Science
Mary.Lacity@umsl.edu

**Professor Leslie Willcocks**
The Outsourcing Unit
The London School of Economics and
Political Science
l.p.willcocks@lse.ac.uk

**Andrew Burgess**
Source
andrew.burgess@source.co.uk

B L O O M S B U R Y
LONDON · NEW DELHI · NEW YORK · SYDNEY

First published in Great Britain 2014

Bloomsbury Publishing Plc
50 Bedford Square
London
WC1B 3DP

www.bloomsbury.com

Bloomsbury Publishing
London, New Delhi, New York and Sydney

A CIP record for this book is available from the British Library.

ISBN: 9-781-472906397

10 9 8 7 6 5 4 3 2 1

Design by Fiona Pike, Pike Design, Winchester
Typeset by Saxon Graphics Ltd, Derby
Printed and bound in Great Britain by CPI Group (UK) Ltd,
Croydon CR0 4YY

# Contents

| | |
|---|---|
| *List of figures* | viii |
| *List of tables* | ix |
| *About the authors* | x |
| *Professional credits* | xii |
| *Acknowledgements* | xiii |
| *Preface* | xiv |

**1. Overview of Legal Services Outsourcing** | **1**
1.1. Introduction | 1
1.2. Bellwether Deals and Test Cases | 3
1.3. Value Proposition | 4
1.4. LSO Challenges | 8
1.5. LSO Learning Curve | 12
1.6. Conclusion | 15

**2. The Provider Landscape** | **19**
2.1. Introduction | 19
2.2. Legal Service Towers | 20
2.3. LSO Provider Pricing | 23
2.4. LSO Revenues | 24
2.5. LSO Provider Size: Headcount | 25
2.6. LSO Staff Turnover | 26
2.7. LSO Provider Geographic Reach | 27
2.8. LSO Provider Team Composition | 27
2.9. LSO Provider Competencies | 29
2.10. Provider Capabilities Model | 32
2.11. Conclusion | 41

**3. Client Perspectives: Recommended Practices** | **43**
3.1. Introduction | 43
3.2. Synopsis of the LSO Case Studies | 46

3.3. LSO Strategy 51
3.4. LSO Provider Selection 55
3.5. Contractual Governance 56
3.6. Stakeholder Buy-in 61
3.7. Transition and Coordination of Work 64
3.8. Provider Turnover 70
3.9. Relational Governance 72
3.10. Location of LSO Staff 75
3.11. Conclusion 77

4. **Navigating the LSO Journey** **79**
4.1. Introduction 79
4.2. Evolution of the Legal Sourcing Model 79
4.3. Legal Process Framework 83
4.4. An Evolutionary Approach: Alternative Journeys 91
4.5. The Legal Ecosystem 97
4.6. Conclusion 102

5. **In Their Own Words** **104**
5.1. Introduction 104
5.2. Christian Sommer, Group Legal Director, Vodafone 106
5.3. Gawie Nienaber, Former Associate GC, CSC 109
5.4. Richard Tapp, Company Secretary and Director
      of Legal Services, Carillion 114
5.5. Mark Harris, CEO, Axiom 118
5.6. Liam Brown, Founder and Chairman,
      Elevate Services 122
5.7. David Holme, Managing Director, Exigent 127
5.8. Bob Gogel, CEO, Integreon 132
5.9. Dan Reed, CEO, UnitedLex 137
5.10. Alex Hamilton, Principal, radiant.law 141
5.11. Conclusion 144

**6. LSO External Benchmarking: Towards High
   Performance**                                              **147**
   6.1. Introduction                                            147
   6.2. Practice 1: Adopt an End-to-End Approach                150
   6.3. Practice 2: Collaborative BPO Governance                153
   6.4. Practice 3: Change Management as Priority               157
   6.5. Practice 4: Seeking Value Beyond Cost                   160
   6.6. Practice 5: Focus on Business Outcomes                  161
   6.7. Practice 6: Domain Expertise and Analytics              164
   6.8. Practice 7: Transformation of the Retained
        Organisation                                            168
   6.9. Practice 8: Technology as Business Enabler              169
   6.10. Conclusion                                             171

**7. LSO Market Predictions**                                   **174**
   7.1. Introduction                                            174
   7.2. Transforming the Shape of Enterprise Legal Functions
        from Pyramids to Diamonds                               175
   7.3. More Panel Reviews and Bundled Services                 176
   7.4. Law Firms will Respond                                  177
   7.5. LSO Providers will Move Up the Value Chain              178
   7.6. New Engagement Models will Emerge                       180
   7.7. LSO Mergers, Acquisitions, and Strategic Alliances      182
   7.8. New Locations will become Competitive                   183
   7.9. Technology will Play an Increasing Role in the
        Provision of Legal Services                             184
   7.10. Conclusion                                             185

**Appendices**                                                  **188**
   A. List of LSO Providers                                     188
   B. Glossary of Terms                                         190

*Index*                                                         193

# Figures

| | | |
|---|---|---|
| 1.1 | The clients outsourcing learning curve | 13 |
| 2.1 | Legal service towers | 21 |
| 2.2 | Skill sets required to perform LSO activities | 22 |
| 2.3 | LSO employee headcount by service tower | 25 |
| 2.4 | LSO employment headcount by geographic location | 28 |
| 2.5 | Average LSO self-assessment by service tower | 30 |
| 2.6 | Average LSO self-assessment by service tower | 31 |
| 2.7 | Resources, capabilities and competencies | 33 |
| 2.8 | Delivery competency | 33 |
| 2.9 | Transformation competency | 34 |
| 2.10 | Relationship competency | 34 |
| 2.11 | Twelve capabilities providers need to develop | 35 |
| 4.1 | Legal process framework | 83 |
| 4.2 | Legal process framework across departments | 84 |
| 4.3 | Managed legal services | 85 |
| 4.4 | Vertical slice of legal activity | 85 |
| 4.5 | Horizontal slice of legal activity | 86 |
| 4.6 | Managed service legal model in detail | 87 |
| 4.7 | Vertical slice of the legal activity model in detail | 89 |
| 4.8 | Horizontal slice of legal activity model in detail | 90 |
| 4.9 | Potential evolutionary outsourcing journeys | 92 |
| 4.10 | Drivers for change | 94 |
| 4.11 | Example legal transformation roadmap | 96 |
| 4.12 | Legal ecosystem | 98 |
| 4.13 | Geographic hub model | 100 |
| 4.14 | Functional hub model | 101 |
| 6.1 | BPO high performance – eight practices | 150 |
| 7.1 | Changing shape of back office functions | 176 |
| 7.2 | LSO work as a function of complexity and criticality | 179 |
| 7.3 | From supplemental staffing to managed services | 181 |

# Tables

2.1  LSO provider daily rates for skill sets                          23
2.2  LSO provider annual revenues from LSO services                  24
2.3  LSO annual staff turnover rates                                 27
2.4  Average team composition                                        29
2.5  Headcount and competency                                        32
3.1  Overview of the LSO relationships                               45
5.1  Thought leaders contributing 'in their own words'              105

# About the authors

**Dr. Mary Lacity** is Curators' Professor of Information Systems and an International Business Fellow at the University of Missouri-St. Louis. She is also Visiting Professor at the London School of Economics and Political Science, a Certified Outsourcing Professional®, Co-Chair of the IAOP Midwest Chapter, Industry Adviser for the Outsourcing Angels, Co-editor of the Palgrave Series *Work, Technology, and Globalization*, and on the Editorial Boards for *Journal of Information Technology, MIS Quarterly Executive, Journal of Strategic Information Systems,* and *Strategic Outsourcing: An International Journal.* She has conducted case studies and surveys of hundreds of organisations on their outsourcing and management practices. She has given executive seminars worldwide and has served as an expert witness for the US Congress. She was the recipient of the 2008 Gateway to Innovation Award sponsored by the IT Coalition, Society for Information Management, and St. Louis RCGA and the 2000 World Outsourcing Achievement Award sponsored by PricewaterhouseCoopers and Michael Corbett and Associates. She has published 15 books, most recently *Advanced Outsourcing Practice: Rethinking ITO, BPO, and Cloud Services* (Palgrave, 2012; co-author Leslie Willcocks). Her publications have appeared in the *Harvard Business Review, Sloan Management Review, MIS Quarterly, IEEE Computer, Communications of the ACM,* and many other academic and practitioner outlets. She was Program Co-chair for ICIS 2010. Before earning her Ph.D. at the University of Houston, she worked as a consultant for Technology Partners International and as a systems analyst for Exxon Company, USA.

**Dr. Leslie Willcocks** has an international reputation for his work on global management, outsourcing, e-business, information management, IT evaluation, strategic IT and organisational change. He is Professor of Technology Work and Globalisation at the Department of

Management at the London School of Economics and Political Science (LSE), and also heads the LSE's Outsourcing Unit. He has been for the last 22 years Editor-in-Chief of the *Journal of Information Technology*. He is co-author of 38 books including most recently *Advanced Outsourcing (2012)* and has published over 220 refereed papers in journals such as *Harvard Business Review, Sloan Management Review, California Management Review, MIS Quarterly* and *MISQ Executive*. He has delivered company executive programmes worldwide, is a regular keynote speaker at international practitioner and academic conferences, and has been retained as adviser and expert witness by major corporations and government institutions. Forthcoming books include *Global Outsourcing Discourse: Exploring Modes of IT Governance* (Palgrave, 2014). His research into the management of cloud business services appears as Willocks, L., Venters, W., and Whitley, E. (2014), *Moving to the Cloud Corporation* (Palgrave, London) (www.outsourcingunit.org).

**Andrew Burgess** is one of the most eminent sourcing consultants in the UK. Whilst working as Consulting Director at Orbys he developed and implemented sourcing strategies for global organisations, running sourcing programmes and helping re-organise IT departments to maximise their value from sourcing. He is considered a leading authority in the growing Legal Transformation and Outsourcing market, working with his clients to help transform legal departments and law firms through the creation of world-class in-house and outsourced capability. He is also a regular speaker at LSO conferences and writes his own LSO blog.

# Professional credits

Portions of Chapter 2, The LPO Provider Landscape, were initially published in Lacity, M., and Willcocks, L. (2013), 'Industry Insight: Legal Process Outsourcing: The Provider Landscape', in *Strategic Outsourcing: An International Journal,* Vol. 6, (2). Reprinted with kind permission from Emerald.

Chapter 3, Client Perspectives: Recommended Practices, was initially published in Lacity, M., and Willcocks, L. (2013). Lacity, M., and Willcocks, L. (2013), "Legal Process Outsourcing, In-house Counsels, Law Firms and Providers: Researching Effective Practices," Web Journal of Current Legal Issues, Vol. 19. Reprinted with kind permission from editor.

The eight high-performing best practices discussed in Chapter 6 are from the authors' research conducted with Accenture and the Everest Group. See Mindrum, C., Hindle, J., Lacity, M., Simonson, E., Sutherland, C., and Willcocks, L. (2012), Achieving High Performance in BPO Research Report available at http://www.accenture.com/microsites/highperfbpo/pages/home.aspx

# Acknowledgements

Firstly, we thank the General Counsels, Partners, CEOs, and many other thought leaders for their time and contributions to this research. These individuals are literally *creating* the LSO landscape. We specifically thank, in alphabetical order, the following people for informing our research: Margaret Blair, Liam Brown, Kevin Colangelo, Leah Cooper, Michael Costello, David Eveleigh, Bob Gogel, Piyush Gupta, Alex Hamilton, Dion Harrington, Mark Harris, Vivek K. Hatti, David Holme, Sven Hool, Rosemary Martin, Ganesh Natarajan, Gawie Nienaber, Peter Nowottny, David Perla, Dan Reed, Mark Ross, Rick Schoeneck, Scott Singer, Christian Sommer, Richard Susskind, Richard Tapp, and Rick Teague. Their insights and generosity have been invaluable in preparing this study.

# Preface

Can outsourcing attack the heart of a profession? In his book *The End of Lawyers?* (OUP, Oxford, revised 2010), Richard Susskind urged legal professionals to ask themselves what elements of their workload could be undertaken more quickly, more cheaply, more efficiently, or to a higher quality using different working methods. For Susskind, this advice was intended to pre-empt the market – a market that is unlikely to tolerate expensive lawyers for tasks that can be better discharged with the support of modern systems and techniques. Susskind believes that the legal profession will be driven by two forces over this decade: by a market pull towards the commoditisation of legal services – in the UK, the legal profession is already facing deregulation – and by the pervasive development and uptake of disruptive technologies. Not surprisingly, these messages have been received with alarm across the globe in a profession that is not known for its propensity for radical change.

If Susskind is correct, where do outsourcing and offshoring fit into this scenario? For the legal profession, the dominant outsourcing model has been called Legal Process Outsourcing (LPO). But as we began researching 'LPO', we learned quickly that too often the 'LPO' nomenclature is used narrowly to refer to the tactical offshoring of low level legal work. While this type of LPO is certainly valuable, it by no means captures the broader landscape of sourcing options, including third party provisioning of end-to-end services. Thus, we titled this book, *The Rise of Legal Services Outsourcing*. Legal Services Outsourcing (LSO) is when a company, organisation, or law firm procures legal services from an external provider. From this definition, the 'external provider' may be located domestically, offshore, or internationally and the 'service' may include any service that supports a legal organisation, from legal support services performed by office workers, IT professionals, and paralegals to complex end-to-end legal services.

The LSO market is growing rapidly as a result of market forces driving enterprise legal functions to transform into leaner organisations. In-house counsels are no longer exempt from the cost-cutting and streamlining imposed on other support functions. This means that enterprise legal functions are seeking ways to reduce costs using a number of different techniques: by opening captive centres in low-cost areas; by pressuring law firms to reduce fees and to be more efficient by offshoring; and by engaging offshore LSO providers directly. Law firms are facing this pressure from their enterprise clients, but also from other customers for whom deregulation is opening up the prospect of shopping for better deals. Ultimately, nearly all legal firms and in-house counsels will have to consider the opportunities and risks of LSO. We wrote this book initially to help educate clients about leveraging value from the emerging global LSO landscape. But as the research progressed we realised the value of our findings to practitioners and senior decision-makers throughout what is now a globalising legal services value chain. We therefore address clients, lawyers, legal firms and service providers, as well as advanced students on courses relating to the global sourcing of business and IT services.

Our overall message is that enterprise legal functions and law firms cannot ignore the fundamental changes to the legal profession caused by globalisation, disruptive technologies, and deregulation: clients must at least *consider* LSO. We acknowledge that there are presently many obstacles to overcome and new competencies to master. But contemporaneous excuses about the profession being an art, that providers from across the world cannot produce quality work, that work cannot be disaggregated, and that the legal profession is not good at project management or processes are the same arguments many Chief Information Officers made about Information Technology

Outsourcing (ITO) in the 1980s and many Chief Financial Officers and Vice Presidents of Human Resources made about Business Process Outsourcing (BPO) in the 1990s. The good news is that many lessons from ITO and BPO apply to LSO, thus learning can be accelerated when General Counsels seek the advice embedded across their own organisations. Lessons to accelerate learning can be gained also from early adopters, many of whom share their deep insights about obtaining value from LSO in each chapter of this book.

Chapter 1 describes the potential value to be gained from LSO services. Although most potential clients focus on the cost advantages of LSO, clients can realise additional value from LSO including the ability to focus in-house legal staff on higher-value work, faster service delivery, scalability, utility pricing, improved service quality, process transformation, access to innovation, and even commercialisation. To obtain such value, however, there are significant challenges to consider and new capabilities to master.

Chapter 2 provides an overview of the LSO landscape. Based on data from 27 LSO providers, we assessed LSO provider services, skill sets and qualifications, scalability of services, geographic reach, pricing, team composition and provider competencies. The sample includes specialist LSO providers, full service LSO providers, and global BPO providers that offer LSO services. The LSO provider landscape changes quickly and provider capabilities must be monitored continually.

Chapter 3 presents effective LSO practices from five successful LSO case studies. Based on in-depth interviews with clients and providers from these LSO relationships, we recommend a range of effective practices to ensure that LSO engagements meet client expectations. The recommended practices pertain to LSO strategy, LSO provider selection, stakeholder-buy-in, contractual governance, transition and co-ordination of work, provider turnover, relational governance, and location of LSO staff. The lessons learned by the five companies in this chapter will be likely re-learned in many other enterprise legal functions as they too explore alternative approaches to sourcing legal services.

Chapter 4 gives a sense of order as to how Legal Service Outsourcing could evolve in organisations to that critical business activity. This chapter seeks to define a common organisational model that can be used to guide the evolutionary journey of legal transformation that will deliver positive outcomes for both clients and service providers.

In previous chapters we analysed, synthesised, and aggregated the lessons from many research participants, but in Chapter 5, we invited nine thought leaders to be heard *in their own words*. We are pleased that leaders from enterprise legal functions, LPO/LSO providers, and an external law firm contributed to this chapter. These individuals are *creating* the LSO landscape. They are constantly adapting its features as lessons are learned and most importantly, as capabilities are built.

In Chapter 6, we provide a set of external benchmarks for legal services to assess themselves against. Based on exhaustive research, the benchmarks establish the eight distinctive management practices adopted by the top 20 per cent performing business process outsourcing arrangements across other sectors such as human resources, procurement, IT, and finance and accounting. And all of these sectors at some stage in their histories considered themselves unique, distinctive, and not open to standardisation, or generic management recipes.

In Chapter 7, we look ahead to assess the trends that are shaping the future of the legal profession. We predict that the shape of enterprise legal functions will increasingly move from 'pyramids' to 'diamonds', with LSO providers performing more work at the base of the pyramid.

But LSO will not remain as 'bottom feeders' and indeed LSO providers are already moving up the value chain. New engagement models are emerging beyond remote staff augmentation and tactical outsourcing. New types of organisations are emerging so that the delineated boundaries of today's three prominent players – enterprise legal functions, law firms, and LSO providers – are blurring. Finally, significant mergers and acquisitions (M&A) and strategic alliance activity will fuel provider growth and capabilities in ways that we cannot wholly foresee today.

 In 2013 Richard Susskind produced an update to his thesis, this time more optimistically called *Tomorrow's Lawyers* (OUP, Oxford). Here he points to major discontinuities already underway for the legal profession, naming three in particular – the 'more-for-less' challenge, liberalisation, and disruptive information technologies. We could not agree more, and the theme of our book – the rise of legal services outsourcing – fits within the context of those three 'disrupters' as both challenge and problem, but also as a potential way forward and opportunity. Using external service providers can be not only counter-cultural but for some activities it can even be unnecessary and counter-productive. But Susskind's three challenges are not going to go away. We have written this book, informed (as it is) over 20 years of research, together with extensive specific examination of legal services, to guide decision-makers and practice towards how external and internal services can be reconstructed, managed effectively and leveraged for superior performance. Not grasping the essentials we provide could, in our view, seriously disadvantage client, legal and provider firm competitiveness in what is now a globalised marketplace.

# Chapter 1

# Overview of Legal Services Outsourcing

## 1.1. Introduction

Nearly all legal firms and in-house counsels will have to consider the opportunities and risks afforded by Legal Services Outsourcing (LSO), the practice of procuring legal services from an external provider. LSO is growing as a result of larger market forces driving enterprise legal functions to transform into leaner organisations.[1] In-house counsels are no longer exempt from the cost cutting and streamlining imposed on all other support functions. Enterprise legal functions are seeking ways to reduce costs by erecting captive centres[2] in low-cost areas, by pressuring major law firms to reduce fees and to be more efficient by offshoring, and by engaging LSO providers directly.[3]

Sizing a market is more art than science. Some sources estimate that the global LSO market was worth $2.4 billion in 2012[4] and will exceed $3 billion by the end of 2013. Growth rate estimates vary considerably from 26 to 28 per cent annually[5] up to 60 per cent.[6] Some sources even suggest that LPO growth stalled in 2011 as law firms reduced fees through their own captive centres.[7] Regardless of its present size, the *potential* global LSO market is enormous. Just considering the US market, the legal services industry is worth about $245 billion, of which 80 per cent is generated from law firms and 20 per cent from in-house counsel. According to First Research, the US market is highly fragmented and includes about 180,000 law offices, with 50 of the largest firms generating only about 15 per cent of revenue.[8] Competition is fierce in fragmented markets and increasingly clients are pushing back against large legal bills, for which prices have increased by 75 per cent (compared to 20 per cent for non-legal business services) in the past decade.[9] In 2011, a survey of in-house counsel heads found that more than half of all respondents use or would consider using offshore legal process outsourcing.[10] LSO is a proven way to reduce costs, which is thus one of the main drivers of LSO market growth. As we discuss in this chapter, the value proposition of LSO is quite alluring and extends beyond cost savings.

Presently, the LSO provider landscape is varied and includes specialty LSO/KPO[11] providers like CPA Global, UnitedLex, Integreon, Mindcrest, Pangea3, and Quislex, and, to a lesser extent, large, global ITO and BPO providers like WNS, Infosys, TCS, and Wipro. Indian-based providers are the leaders in the offshore LSO space, with more than one million lawyers and 128 LSO providers exporting legal services worth $640 million in 2010.[12] Indian's LSO market may grow to $4 billion by 2015.[13] The Philippines, often considered the second largest LSO offshore destination after India, has 40,000 lawyers.[14] But the LSO provider landscape is changing swiftly, with mergers, acquisitions and divestitures. New model firms are emerging that are blending the traditional law firm model with rural and offshore delivery models. Potential LSO clients need a way to navigate this landscape that mediates risks while still deriving value.

Given LSO's strong value proposition and huge market potential, clients with little or no LSO experience will want to learn more. The Outsourcing Unit at the London School of Economics and Political Science, in collaboration with legal sourcing consultant Andrew Burgess, launched a research project to help educate and disseminate learning about LSO. The research comprises detailed data on 27 LSO providers and in-depth interviews with LSO clients, providers, and advisers. In addition to the LSO specific research, we have been studying Information Technology Outsourcing (ITO) since 1989 and Business Process Outsourcing (BPO) since 2000. Many client experiences with LSO echo the client experiences with ITO and BPO, and therefore lessons from ITO and BPO can give context to and help educate and inform LSO users. Of course there are distinctive LSO challenges which we detail below, but the main purpose of this book is to help accelerate the learning curve for in-house counsels and law firms who have yet to begin, or are in the early phases of adopting LSO.

## 1.2. Bellwether deals and test cases

LSO may also be compared to ITO and BPO in that the industry is being created 'on the backs of deals'.[15] Bellwether deals certainly have legitimated the adoption of LSO. In 2009, in a well-publicised deal, the global mining company Rio Tinto engaged Indian LSO provider CPA Global and saved $8 million per year, a fifth of its legal costs.[16] Leah Cooper, Managing Attorney at Rio Tinto, became a celebrity in legal circles for this decision in the same way Kathy Hudson, CIO of Kodak, became a celebrity in 1989 for her bellwether Information Technology Outsourcing (ITO) deal with IBM, BusinessLand, and DEC. Although both Cooper's and Hudson's deals were not the first LSO or ITO contracts, the deals were big enough and bold enough to gain worldwide attention. Soon after Rio Tinto's LSO decision, other major LSO deals warranted headlines. In March 2010, BT signed a three-year, $5 million deal with UnitedLex to provide commercial contracting and antitrust regulation services. In May 2010, UK law firm Cameron McKenna signed a £583 million, ten-year deal with Integreon, an LSO and business process outsourcing (BPO) provider based in the US with delivery centres in India, the Philippines, China and South Africa.[17] In June 2010, Microsoft signed a three-year, $20 million contract with Wipro to provide intellectual property services.[18]

Although bellwether deals and the global economic recession of 2008 have magnified the attention on LSO services, LSO is a long-standing practice. As far back as 1969, for example, Computer Patent Annuities (CPA) was founded by UK patent attorneys to provide intellectual property services, specialising in patent renewals. According to the *Black Book of Outsourcing*, offshoring of legal services dates back to the mid-1990s, when large companies like Bickel Brewer LLP and General Electric erected captive centres in India. Although captive centres are not technically LSO because the client directly employs the offshore staff, the offshoring of captive centres provided the necessary test cases that allowed transborder LSO to exist in the first place. Despite initial opposition, the American Bar Association agreed that offshore LSO was a salutary practice for a globalised economy in 2008.[19] In the UK, the Legal Services Act of 2007 opened the dialogue for alternative business structures like LSO.[20] With the green light from two of the largest legal markets – the US and UK – the LSO market grew rapidly.

## 1.3. Value proposition

Clients are initially attracted to LSO because of the potential for cost savings. Indeed, the clients we interviewed for this book report total cost savings between 30 per cent and 50 per cent. But LSO has a much richer value proposition than just cost reduction. Clients can realise additional value from LSO services, including the ability to focus in-house legal staff on higher-value work, faster service delivery, scalability, utility pricing, improved service quality, process transformation, access to innovation, and even commercialisation. Each source of value is discussed further below.

**Cost savings.** Firstly, clients value LSO for its cost savings. Whilst a lawyer in major legal markets such as the US may charge from $150 to $350 per hour when performing services, LSO providers may charge between $25 and $50 per hour, depending on the skill level. LSO providers reduce client costs through superior technologies, process maturity, and by substituting high-cost labour for lower-cost labour. Many LSO providers have delivery centres located in low-cost countries like India or the Philippines. From our sample of 27 LSO providers, we calculated the average cost for a fully qualified lawyer based in India at $248 per day (see Chapter 2 for more detail). Offshore LSO prices are lower because salaries are lower. In London, for example, paralegals earn between £30,000 and £44,000 a year compared to £5,000 to £8,000 in the Philippines. London-based lawyers with three years of post-qualification experience earn £75,000 to £86,000 compared to £10,000 to £15,000 in the Philippines.[21] The total cost savings, however, will not be the difference between onshore and offshore salaries, which appear to promise upwards of 600 per cent savings. A more realistic expectation of total cost savings is 30 per cent to 50 per cent. Calculations of total cost savings should include knowledge transfer costs, lost productivity, and most importantly, onshore provider oversight. Most LSO providers employ onshore resources, which are needed for deep customer understanding and to co-ordinate offshore employees.[22] In addition, US- and UK-based clients are demanding more onshore resources, which has prompted offshore LSO providers to hire more onshore lawyers. For example, Integreon opened an LSO delivery centre in Bristol UK in 2012 because, as the Global Head of LSO announced, *As the delivery of legal services evolves, it's clear that most law firms and corporate counsel require a mix of onshore and offshore support.'*[23] Thus, the total cost savings must also consider the investments needed to protect quality, like onshore resources.

**Focus in-house lawyers on more strategic work.** In Richard Susskind's working paper, 'Provocations and Perspectives'[24] he discusses the fallacy of giving junior lawyers low level work under the banner of 'training'. He writes that young lawyers are asked to spend months reviewing documents in preparation for litigation or in a due diligence exercise, but that they master the task in a couple of days. One value of LSO, therefore, is handing off more routine work to providers so that in-house lawyers can focus on more strategic work. In Chapter 3, we present several case studies in which the General Counsels adopted LSO precisely for this reason; they wanted their in-house lawyers to focus on more value-added and more interesting work.

**Increase delivery speed.** Service delivery speed can increase with LSO. For example, Microsoft reports that Integreon increased contract turnaround by 20 per cent and increased on-time delivery of contracts to 99.5 per cent.[25] Service speed can increase by having more people working on a service and by having offshore resources working shifts while Western-based clients are asleep. Achieving a smooth 'follow the sun' work schedule is possible, but requires considerable co-ordination.[26]

**Scalability.** Scalability can be improved by hiring an LSO provider to meet short-term increases in demand. One client we interviewed, for example, uses an LSO provider to help with large document reviews. The LSO provider astonished its client by ramping up with 150 qualified lawyers within a month's notice. The client said, *'If you look at eDiscovery and document review in particular, the volume of work is so spiky. I am very happy for the provider to manage that risk and be able to staff up and ramp down.'*

**Utility pricing.** Besides charging for services by hourly or daily rates, many LSO providers also charge by the unit of work – per contract, per patent, per page, and per project – allowing more predictable bills for clients and a pay-as-you-use model. The challenge is to find the right price so that providers can deliver a quality utility service while still earning a decent profit margin. In our BPO research, we found that utility prices sometimes had to be re-negotiated because the providers were losing money on some deals. Clients must care about protecting the provider's margin to protect quality, to discourage turnover (no provider employee wants to work on a losing account), to foster good relationships, and to make sure the provider does not go out of business.

**Improve quality.** Many clients may assume that an LSO provider's quality will be lower than work performed by in-house staff, but some clients we interviewed report that quality *improved* with outsourcing. With LSO, work products may be more rigorously tracked and most LSO providers have superior technologies for improving services compared to enterprise legal functions. For example, one client said his LSO provider better tracks contract obligations, and found instances when the client was continuing to pay vendors on expired contracts.

**Additional value.** Clients can also consider how LSO might drive other business objectives like process transformation, access to innovation (particularly IT-enabled innovations), access to new markets, and commercialisation (e.g. setting up an LSO business with a provider).[27] According to David Perla, former Co-CEO of Pangea3, an LSO with 850 globally located employees, *'We help transform how work is done in legal departments or large law firms. We do things for clients that they have never done before, such as deploying contract management lifecycle systems or combining legal and technical teams by having lawyers and engineers working side-by-side for many years.'*

**Spur competition.** Finally, nothing beats complacency like healthy competition. Adding an LSO provider to the panel of external legal firms can incentivise all partners to find innovative ways to lower costs or to improve client services. In the US, for example, an excess supply of law school graduates in some cities has enabled mid-cost, domestic delivery centres that offer lower costs compared to established law firms but easier engagements compared to Indian-based providers. In some cases, clients reported that their external legal firms reduced their fees immediately to prevent the client from engaging an LSO provider. In other instances, the law firms welcomed the LSO provider and continued to engage them on other client accounts as a way to differentiate their services.

The promises for extracting value from LSO are certainly compelling, but there are also several major challenges to consider.

## 1.4. LSO Challenges

The fact that the legal sourcing market exists at all is a testament to the benefits that can be achieved from it, for the challenges that it faces are undoubtedly the most severe of any area of outsourcing. There are the generic challenges and risks that any outsourcing programme would need to face, such as the level of change required, the transition to an external provider, the additional governance required and the potential movement or loss of jobs. The legal outsourcing market though, has all these and more. Some of these challenges are inherent to the legal sector:

**Heightened risk averseness.** Lawyers, by the very nature of the work that they do, are risk averse; they are employed to manage the risk of the organisation or client, and so it is no surprise that this state of mind permeates the aspects of how they actually carry out their job. And whilst that can be a very good thing, it should not get in the way of open thinking and acceptance of new ideas.

**Jurisdictional requirements.** Some legal work is specific to certain jurisdictions, meaning that matters and/or data cannot be taken out of the home country. This obviously limits the level of offshoring that can be carried out for these tasks.

**Lack of process maturity.** Many corporate departments, but especially IT departments, have been able to define the work that they do in specific processes and frameworks, such as the Information Technology Infrastructure Library (ITIL). And whilst legal work can also be mapped into processes, this is currently the exception rather than the rule. Part of this is due to the fact that no one has really asked them to do it on an industrial scale, but also because of a certain mindset which says that legal work cannot be defined into processes as it is too variable and unpredictable (how can you write a process for a multi-million pound contract negotiation?).

**Limitations from consensus management.** Specifically relating to law firms, the partnership structure does not necessarily encourage a strategic 'helicopter' view when it comes to addressing large shifts in the market – instead there is a tendency to focus on what a lawyer's specific clients are telling them without necessarily aggregating these views across the firm. If these views do actually get some visibility across the firm, the partnership structure's consensus decision-making process can slow down or inhibit key changes that could positively impact the whole organisation.

**Qualification requirements.** There are obviously strict regulations in place to prohibit the unauthorised practice of law, and all LSO providers must adhere to these. Recent developments with Alternative Business Structures (ABSs) give some freedom but there is still an extremely large threshold between processing legal transactions and practicing law.

**Provider market structure.** The traditional outsourcing market has typically involved a buyer of the services (the client) and a provider of the services (the provider). The legal market has the complexity of including three main parties: the client, the LSO provider and the law firm. This is further complicated by the fact that the law firm can be both a buyer and provider of legal services. The recent changes in some jurisdictions that allow non-lawyers to own law firms further complicates the picture in that some companies that would normally be considered as clients of legal services can now become providers.

Some of the challenges in the legal outsourcing market are the result of how the market itself has developed, and is developing. Let's look at these:

**Predominantly an offshore model.** The IT outsourcing market initially developed with providers providing services on-site or within the same country as their clients, and then moved offshore (mainly to India) to reap additional labour arbitrage benefits. Because the LSO market developed later on, it skipped the initial onshore stage and was, effectively, born offshore. This gave significant benefits in terms of labour costs and the availability of the necessary process and technology skills. However, this also added elements of risk into a model that was already viewed as pretty risky by potential clients. It also, as mentioned above, put some limitations on what work could be done outside of the client's jurisdiction.

**Tactical projects.** The initial driver for LSO services was the eDiscovery requirements in the US which are, inherently, project-based pieces of work. This has led to a bias for distinct and tactical outsourcing projects (with a start and an end) rather than longer term 'strategic' outsourcing deals (to provide ongoing services). That trend has, to date, tended to hold back the market from delivering its full potential as a true outsourcing capability for clients.

**Focus on cost reduction.** Cost reduction can be a significant outcome from legal outsourcing, and is often cited by providers as the primary benefit. However, from a client point of view it can (unjustly) also be seen as having negative connotations, particularly in relation to quality and risk.

**Continual market development and maturing.** A characteristic of any relatively new market is that the rate of change will be high, and this is very true in the LSO market right now. Influences such as a maturing and consolidating provider market, regulatory changes and economic cycles will ensure that the market will not stand still for years to come.

**Relatively small provider base.** There are very capable LSO providers in the market, but, compared to other areas of Business Process Outsourcing (BPO), the numbers and size of the providers are small – this limits choice for clients and introduces risk if there is a mis-match in size between the client and provider. Additionally, many of these providers are still funded by private equity which imposes certain drivers and motivations on to the organisation that may not be aligned with those of their clients.

**Specialist technologies.** The use of technology in law firms and legal departments tends to be ad-hoc and limited in application. Partly this is due to the specialist nature of the work, but also to the legal technology market which is currently fragmented and siloed. The lack of any real industry-wide standards inhibits the adoption of technology, and the general use of 'cloud' technologies creates further issues with regard to data confidentiality.

**Lack of data and experience.** A new market will have little experience and data to guide it, and this is particularly true of the LSO market. Whereas benchmarking is a mature activity in IT, it would currently be extremely difficult (unless at a very high level) in LSO.

And, because everyone learns from their mistakes, a nascent market has less experience to help it develop and mature.

## 1.5. LSO learning curve

Outsourcing has a significant learning curve[28]. Figure 1.1 illustrates the typical client learning curve for outsourcing we found from studying ITO and BPO and now LSO. During Phase 1, clients become aware of outsourcing through marketing hype ('you'll shave 50 per cent off your costs') or irrational propaganda ('we'll lose all our intellectual property'). Clients quickly learn about potential benefits, costs, and risks by talking to peers, advisers, and reading the research. Most clients initially begin outsourcing with pilot projects to reduce costs on a few targeted projects (Phase 2). Clients often make mistakes in this phase, such as focusing the deal so tightly on costs that they fail to invest enough resources to ensure quality service. They might also have picked a poor provider in terms of matching the provider's capabilities with client needs. They may size projects so small that the high transaction costs of knowledge transfer, work co-ordination and management oversight erode all the labour cost savings. In these circumstances, the business case evaporates and the extra headache of dealing with a third-party provider can sour an organisation on outsourcing. Good pilot projects, in contrast, thoroughly test the LSO concept. One General Counsel, for example, measured the quality of work for *every work product* coming out of India during a three month pilot. After the trial period, he was convinced that the provider's employees were very competent. Another enterprise legal function pitted two LSO providers against each other by assigning them exactly the same work to determine the superior performer.

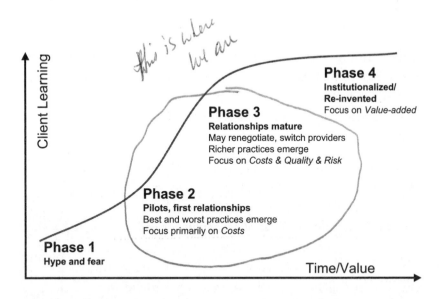

*this is where we are*

**Figure 1.1: The Client's Outsourcing Learning Curve**

As learning accumulates from initial LSO engagements, clients move to Phase 3 when they have a more balanced emphasis on cost, quality, risks, and speed of delivery (i.e. not just cost). Clients have learned better what it takes to make outsourcing work in terms of retained client capabilities and better contractual and relational governance. Fully mature outsourcing clients reach Phase 4; as of yet, we have not encountered any LSO clients claiming this level of maturity. For ITO and BPO clients, we find two prominent routes in Phase 4. Some mature adopters in Phase 4 use outsourcing to strategically enable corporate strategies, such as increasing business agility, bringing products to market faster and cheaper, financing new product development, accessing new markets, or creating new business. Other mature adopters have 'institutionalised' outsourcing in that they have a strong internal procurement function and a team of in-house advisers that manage a portfolio of outsourcing relationships. Outsourcing is an accepted and expected practice for non-core capabilities.

*legal procurement is a mature function*

This learning curve captures the experiences of thousands of organisations we have studied. The main lesson is that even false starts and mis-steps early in the learning curve can produce powerful lessons that enable clients to outsource successfully. What do clients need to learn and how is learning accelerated?

**Client Capabilities.** Our ITO and BPO research[29] has found that clients must learn to change their management practices after outsourcing in order to achieve the anticipated benefits from outsourcing. Clients must become good at managing providers by shifting their capabilities from managing resources and processes to managing inputs and outputs. This is not an easy transition for many clients. The supplier management capability was often found to be lacking in client organisations and seen as a major reason to explain negative outsourcing outcomes. Supplier management is much more than holding providers accountable to a contract. Instead it requires strong relational governance with high levels of communication, transparency, knowledge sharing, joint problem solving, and trust. Technical and methodological capability was the second most frequently important client retained capability, particularly in the ITO literature. Technical and methodological capability is an operational capability needed by both parties in order to co-ordinate work effectively. A client also needs to be able to identify, rate, and mitigate potential risks associated with outsourcing (risk management capability). Researchers have studied the effects of a client's ability to manage a business process themselves and found that clients are more likely to successfully outsource a business process that they can manage efficiently and effectively themselves. This finding resonates with the maxim that if you 'outsource your mess for less' you will only get cost reduction, but little, and probably no improvement in anything else. Clients must learn to understand, accept, and adapt to cultural differences between themselves and their providers (cultural distance management capability). Other client capabilities have also been identified as affecting outsourcing decisions and outcomes: client outsourcing readiness, transition management capability, and change management capability.[30]

**Provider Capabilities.** Which provider capabilities contribute to positive outsourcing outcomes? Our ITO and BPO research[31] found that the most important provider firm capabilities were human resource management capability, technical and methodological capability, and domain understanding. A provider's ability to identify, acquire, develop, and deploy human resources to achieve both provider's and client's organisational objectives was found to positively and significantly affect client outcomes 95 per cent of the time it was examined. Clients often engage providers because of their superior human resources in terms of both number and quality of staff. The provider's technical and methodological capability was the second most frequently studied capability and it was found to affect outcomes positively (see above). Domain understanding is the extent to which a provider has prior experience and/or understanding of the client organisation's business and technical contexts, processes, practices, and requirements. Other provider capabilities were also found to be important: client management capability, managing client expectations, risk management capability, security, privacy and confidentiality capability, and corporate social responsibility capability. Providers are unlikely to excel in all of these areas, but better capabilities lead to better outcomes.[32]

## 1.6 Conclusion

Like all outsourcing practices, outsourcing of legal services is not about abdicating responsibility, but rather about learning how to manage in a different way. Clients have a significant learning curve to ride, but learning can be accelerated. Within an organisation, learning can be promoted with good pilot projects and by seeking insights from other back offices that have already externally sourced services. Outside an organisation, early adopters can teach us about the best and worst practices for engaging LSO providers. LSO providers also have important insights to share, and specialist advisers can reduce the risks of the outsourcing journey. In the chapters that follow, our aim is to share what we have learned from early adopters, LSO providers, and advisers during our research project. One might reasonably ask, 'Is all this effort worthwhile?' The answer is a resounding 'yes' because the forces of globalisation, technology enablement, disaggregation of work, process standardisation, and deregulation will shift the legal landscape whether we welcome these forces or not.

---

1    Wood, L., (2011), 'Research and Markets: The Global LPO Market is Expected to be Worth $2.4 billion in 2012', *Business Wire*, March 11; see also the *Black Book of Outsourcing: 2010 Leading Providers of Legal Process Outsourcing*. See Susskind, R. (2008), *The End of Lawyers? Rethinking the Nature of Legal Services*, Oxford University Press, Oxford; Gulian, C., 'Tightened Client Budgets Fuel Need for Outsourcing', *Rochester Business Journal*, Vol. 28, 2012.

2    This chapter focuses on Legal Services Outsourcing, but many readers may also want to consider captive centres. Oshri, I. (2011), *Offshoring Strategies: Evolving Captive Center Models*, MIT Press, Cambridge, MA is highly recommended as a source.

3    Lacity, M., and Willcocks, L. (2013), 'Industry Insight: Legal Process Outsourcing: The Provider Landscape', *Strategic Outsourcing: An International Journal*, Vol. 5, (2), forthcoming; Orbys (2010), *Legal Outsourcing: Current Market Trends*, Reference Code DMTC2399.

4    Wood, L., (2011), 'Research and Markets: The Global LPO Market is Expected to be Worth $2.4 billion in 2012', *Business Wire*, 11th March; see also, the *Black Book of Outsourcing: 2010 Leading Providers of Legal Process Outsourcing*.

5    'Research and Markets: The LPO Market in India to Grow at a CAGR of 27.5%', *Business Wire*, 8th March, 2012; Deloitte, *The Resurgence of Corporate Legal Processing: Leveraging a New and Improved Legal Support Business Model*, 2011, available online.

6    Source: Wikipedia.

7    Griffins, C. (2012), 'LPOver and Out?' *The Lawyer*, 22nd October, p. 16.

8    First Research, Legal Services Industry Profile, 2012, see http://www.firstresearch.com/Industry-Research/Legal-Services.html (accessed July 2013).

9    Harris, M. (2012), 'Why More Law Firms Will Go the Way of Dewey & LeBoeuf', *Forbes*, 8th
     May, www.forbes.com/sites/forbesleadershipforum/2012/05/08/why-more-law-firms-will-go-
     the-way-of-dewey-leboeuf/.

10   'Law Department Operations Survey Results' in *PR Newswire*, 19th Jan, 2012.

11   Knowledge Process Outsourcing (KPO) is the outsourcing of processes that require highly
     specialised knowledge or expertise, such as medical, product design, animation, medical, and
     legal processes. From this definition, LPO may be viewed as a subset of KPO.

12   Wood, L. (2010), 'Research and Markets: Indian Legal Process Outsourcing Market', *Business
     Wire*, 7th October.

13   Wood, L. (2010), op. cit.

14   'Legal Process Outsourcing Is as Much About Efficiency as Cost-Cutting.' *Layer2B*, 2011, Vol. 7.

15   Quote credited to Matt Shocklee, Global Ambassador for the International Association of
     Outsourcing Professionals (IAOP).

16   'Passage to India: The Growth of Legal Outsourcing', *The Economist*, 26th June, 2010; 'First LPO
     Conference Creates Debate', *The Lawyer*, 2009, Vol. 4.

17   Ibid.

18   http://www.wipro.com/newsroom/Wipro-Partners-with-Microsoft-to-Deliver-Global-Legal-
     Process-Outsourcing-Efficiencies (accessed July 2013).

19   Lin, A. (2008), 'ABA Gives Thumbs Up to Legal Outsourcing', *New York Law Journal*, 27th
     August.

20   http://www.legislation.gov.uk/ukpga/2007/29/contents (accessed July 2013).

21   'Legal Process Outsourcing Is as Much About Efficiency as Cost-Cutting.' *Layer2B*, 2011, Vol. 7.

22   A Study by Fronterion in 2010 found that 44 per cent of LPO providers were increasing their
     onshore personnel, primarily because US and UK clients were reticent to send work directly
     offshore. According to the source 'Why Too Much Onshoring Could Create a Headache for LPO
     providers', *The Lawyer*, 2010, LPO providers that increase onshore staff *'operate on the assumption
     that eventually most of their domestic work will be sent abroad.'*

23   'Integreon Opens Onshore LPO Delivery Center in Bristol', *Business Wire*, 27th January, 2012.

24   Susskind, R. 'Provocations and Perspectives'. A Working Paper submitted to UK CLE Research
     Consortium, October 2012.

25   'Microsoft Utilizes Integreon LPO Services to Gain Efficiencies while Reducing Costs', *Business
     Wire*, 6th April, 2010.

26   Carmel, E. and Espinosa, A. (2011), *I'm Working while They're Sleeping: Time Zone Separation
     Challenges and Solutions*, Nedder Stream Press, US.

27   For more strategic business objectives achieved with outsourcing see: DiRomualdo, A. and
     Gurbaxani, V. (1998). 'Strategic Intent for IT Outsourcing', *Sloan Management Review*, Vol.39, (4),
     pp. 67–80; Lacity, M., Feeny, D. and Willcocks, L. (2004), 'Commercializing the Back Office at
     Lloyds of London: Outsourcing and strategic partnerships revisited', *European Management Journal*,
     Vol. 22, (2), pp. 127–40; Van Gorp, D., Jagersma, P. and Livshits, A. (2007), 'Offshore Behavior
     of Service Firms: Policy implications for firms and nations', *Journal of Information Technology Cases
     and Application Research*, Vol. 9, (1), pp. 7–19.

28   Lacity, M. and Rottman, J. (2008), *Offshore Outsourcing of IT Work*, Palgrave, United Kingdom.

29  Lacity, M., Khan, S., Yan, A., and Willcocks, L. (2010), 'A Review of the IT Outsourcing Empirical Literature and Future Research Directions', *Journal of Information Technology*, Vol. 25, (4), pp. 395–433;  Lacity, M., Solomon, S., Yan, A., and Willcocks, L. (2011), "Business Process Outsourcing Studies: A Critical Review and Research Directions," *Journal of Information Technology*, Vol. 26, 4, pp. 221-258.

30  Lacity *et al.* 2010; 2011, op. cit.

31  Lacity, M., Khan, S., Yan, A., and Willcocks, L. (2010), 'A Review of the IT Outsourcing Empirical Literature and Future Research Directions', *Journal of Information Technology*, Vol. 25, (4), pp. 395–433;  Lacity, M., Solomon, S., Yan, A., and Willcocks, L. (2011), "Business Process Outsourcing Studies: A Critical Review and Research Directions," *Journal of Information Technology*, Vol. 26, 4, pp. 221-258.

32  Lacity *et al.* 2010; 2011, op. cit.

# Chapter 2

# The Provider Landscape

## 2.1. Introduction

In this chapter, we analyse LSO provider data collected by a leading sourcing and transformation advisory firm based in Europe. The 27 providers in the sample include specialist LSO providers, full service LSO providers, and global BPO providers that offer LSO services. We assessed LSO provider services, provider competencies, geographic location, pricing, team composition, and staff turnover rates.

To interpret the data collected, we first present an LSO framework that defines the scope of LSO services. This framework in itself will be helpful to potential LSO clients as it captures the full range of the LSO services and skill sets. Next, we present the analyses and findings on LSO providers, including the employee headcount by service tower and by geographic location, a self-assessment of provider competency by service and service tower, the mix of onshore and offshore resources for an average LSO engagement, the average prices by skill level and location, and average turnover rates. We conclude with implications for current and future LSO clients.

Across the sample, the 27 LSO providers employ a total of 10,858 LSO workers. The smallest firm in the sample employed 25 people, the largest firm employed 2,000 people, and the average number of LSO employees was 402. These figures only include LSO employees, not employees devoted to other service areas such as ITO or BPO. The average LSO revenue was $35,187,454 in 2011, but we only had LSO revenue data for 14 LSO providers. LSO revenue data is difficult to capture because some LSO providers cannot isolate LSO revenues from their overall BPO revenues, some LSO providers are private companies and have policies against disclosure, and some LSO providers are just starting up.

## 2.2. **Legal service towers**

What services do LSO providers perform? We conceive of the entire suite of LSO as comprising ten service towers (see Figure 2.1). Seven towers support traditional legal activities:

**Tower 1.** *Litigation Services* – discovery, document, and case management services;

**Tower 2.** *Intellectual Property Services* – patents, trademarks, and domain name services;

**Tower 3.** *Corporate Services* – mergers and acquisitions, transaction agreements, and corporate financing services;

**Tower 4.** *Compliance Services* – regulatory and company policy compliance services;

**Tower 5.** *Services Procurement* – contracts, service agreements, and outsourcing services;

**Tower 6.** *Employment Services* – employment contracts, disputes, immigration and injury services;

**Tower 7.** *Property Services* – purchase, lease, rent, or sale of physical property.

Three towers provide supporting services:

**Tower 8.** *Resourcing* – staff augmentation, including administrative, paralegal, and legal staffing;

**Tower 9.** *Consulting Services* – high-level consulting on strategy, transformation, policy, and procedures;

**Tower 10.** *Bundled services* – information technology, business process, and knowledge process services that complement or support LSO services.

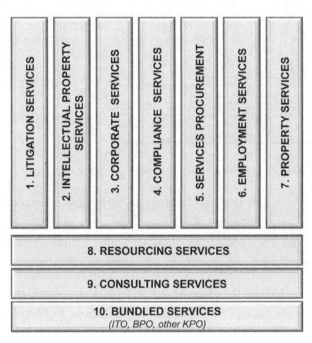

*Figure 2.1: Legal Service Towers*

Common legal activities are performed within each of the seven main service towers, such as researching, drafting and managing documents, preparing matters, performing legal and commercial analyses, providing legal advice, taking legal action, and managing legal and non-legal services (see Appendix B for definitions). Different skill levels and qualifications are needed to perform these common activities (see Figure 2.2):

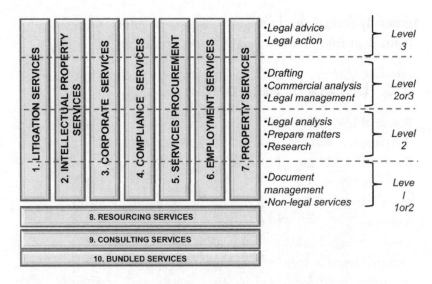

*Figure 2.2: Skill sets Required to Perform LSO Activities*

**Level 1:** Activities that can be done by generalist resources, such as secretarial or administrative staff and therefore do not require any specific legal knowledge. People with Level 1 skills are qualified to perform non-legal and document management services.

**Level 2:** Activities that require some legal knowledge and context but do not necessarily require legal qualifications to carry them out, such as legal analysis, matter preparation, and legal analysis. Depending on the complexity of the activity, people with Level 2 skills may also be qualified to perform drafting, commercial analysis, and legal management services.

**Level 3:** Activities that are of high value require at least some legal qualifications to carry out. People with Level 3 skills are qualified to provide legal advice and to take legal actions; people with Level 3 skills may be needed to perform complex drafting, commercial analysis, and legal management services. These activities, though, generally exclude the 'legal opinion' normally provided by senior in-house counsels and external law firms.

## 2.3. LSO provider pricing

Potential LSO clients are interested in the would-be cost savings, and therefore will want to compare their own daily rates for skill sets with those of LSO providers. We analysed daily rates for Level 1 (administrative), Level 2 (paralegal) and Level 3 (technical legal specialists and fully qualified lawyers). The range of prices is very wide (see Table 2.1). For example, the daily prices for fully qualified lawyers range from $160 to $2,000 per day. The average of $530 includes averages from all locations. We have price data specifically for India-based staff from ten providers, and these averages are considerably lower than the averages across all locations.

| Skill level | Low | High | Average overall (all locations; n = 26) | Average (India only; n = 10) |
|---|---|---|---|---|
| (1) Administrative | $60 | $320 | $201 | n/a |
| (2) Paralegal | $75 | $400 | $249 | $176 |
| (3) Technical | $160 | $2,800 | $342 | $183 |
| (3) Fully qualified lawyer | $160 | $2,000 | $530 | $248 |

*Table 2.1: LSO provider daily rates for skill sets (One day = eight hours)*

While many LSO providers can provide daily rates for these skill sets, a number of LSO providers do not normally bill by time spent, but instead create teams with blended rates or price based on output to be delivered. One provider explained the use of blended rates; *'We do not typically charge fees based on resource type or level. Rather, we provide a blended fee for a specific service to include management time, project management, quality management and reporting, etc. The exact composition of resources will depend upon the exact nature of the services required and will be identified during a detailed scoping exercise that is undertaken at the early stage of any engagement.'* Another LSO provider describes their output-based pricing: *'We rarely use resource-based pricing (hourly, daily, weekly or otherwise). Instead, we prefer to use output-based pricing because it better aligns incentives between [LSO provider] and its clients. Billing on a time and materials basis penalises the provider for investing in efficiency and productivity, which would reduce the amount of billable time. As we view our ability to deliver efficiency and productivity gains as a core strength, we prefer to bill on an output-based model that rewards us for productivity gains while passing on most of the gains to clients in the form of lower cost per unit of work.'*

## 2.4. LSO provider revenues

Data on LSO revenues is difficult to capture because (1) some LSO providers cannot isolate LSO revenues from their overall BPO revenues, (2) some LSO providers are private companies and have policies against disclosure, and (3) some LSO providers are just starting up. We were able to analyse LSO revenues for 14 LSO providers based on data held by the consulting firm. The 2010 average revenue for 14 LSO providers was $36.5 million (see Table 2.2). The 2011 average revenue was lower than the 2010 average by $1.3 million, perhaps because the data was collected in the fourth quarter of 2011 and not all revenues were reported or perhaps because the market indeed dipped.

|  | 2008 | 2009 | 2010 | 2011 |
|---|---|---|---|---|
| Average revenues | $10,392,500 | $28,403,529 | $36,535,196 | $35,187,454 |

*Table 2.2: LSO provider annual revenues from LSO services (n = 14)*

## 2.5. LSO provider size: headcount

Based on headcount data, we were able to analyse the total number of employees devoted to LSO services for 27 providers. As a group, the 27 LSO providers employ a total of 10,858[*] LSO workers. The smallest firm in the sample employed 25 people and the largest firm employed 2,000 people in 2011. The average number of LSO employees was 402.

The data also captured LSO employee headcount across the nine LSO service towers (see Figure 2.3). Among the nine service towers, litigation represents the highest percentage of LSO employee headcount, representing 26 per cent of the 10,858 employees in the sample. Intellectual property is the second largest populated service tower at 14 per cent. LSO consulting is the smallest populated service tower, representing 1 per cent of the sample. We note that many LSO providers cross-train staff so that an employee can perform work in several service towers.

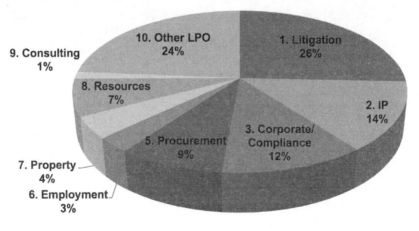

*Figure 2.3: LSPO Employee Headcount by Service Tower*

---

[*]   These figures only include LSO employees, not employees devoted to other service areas such as ITO or BPO.

## 2.6. **LSO staff turnover**

High staff turnover in low-cost countries has been a major problem for ITO and BPO providers and clients. Turnover rates for ITO and BPO in India have been as high as 60 per cent, with an industry average of 20 per cent to 30 per cent per year.[1] High provider staff turnover delays the clients' projects, reduces quality, and increases costs.[2] Do LSO providers suffer from similarly high turnover rates?

Based on turnover data for 17 LSO providers, the overall average turnover rate is 15 per cent (see Table 2.3). The range of turnover rates varies considerably across LSO providers, spanning 3 per cent to 34 per cent. The LSO provider reporting a 3 per cent turnover rate employs 450 people, which is quite an astonishingly low turnover rate. The provider indicates: *'The current retention rate for employees in India is 96.8 per cent. We do not include associates who leave or are dismissed prior to their confirmation in this calculation. The majority of our employees have been with us for more than three years. All our managers based in India have been with us for four plus years. Our management team is characterised by longevity and continuity that is not typically seen in this industry. Our annual attrition rate is historically in the single digits.'* The highest reported turnover rate was 60 per cent for Level 3 resources. However, this rate is explained by the LSO provider's business model: *'Turnover rate for Level 3 is due to the contractual nature of the projects. Specific attorneys are contracted for specialised matters and may be used infrequently.'*

LSO providers have lower turnover rates compared to ITO and BPO providers in India, but higher turnover rates compared to ITO and BPO providers in Eastern Europe, which have an average turnover rate of 10 per cent, and in the US, for which the average IT turnover rate is only 5.5 per cent.[3] LSO providers have turnover rates comparable to China's turnover rates, which average between 7.5 per cent and 15 per cent.

| | Level 1 skills (n=5) | Level 2 skills (n=6) | Level 3 skills (n=7) | Overall (n = 17) |
|---|---|---|---|---|
| Range | 7%–20% | 0%–30% | 0%–60% | 3%–34% |
| Average | 11% | 11% | 12% | 15% |

*Table 2.3: LSO annual staff turnover rates*

## 2.7. LSO provider geographic reach

We analysed LSO headcount by geographic location. Among the 10,858* LSO workers employed by the 27 LSO providers in the sample, India is the most common location of LSO staff, representing 59 per cent of the sample (see Figure 2.4). The US is the second most common location, with 22 per cent of the LSO provider headcount. In the 'Other' category, LSO providers have employees based in China, Hong Kong, Latin America, Singapore, South Africa, and Sri Lanka.

## 2.8. LSO provider team composition

In order for LSO providers to reduce costs for their clients and still protect service quality, they balance onshore and offshore resources. Onshore resources are more expensive but have the advantages of close customer proximity, deep domain understanding, and high cultural compatibility. Offshore resources are less expensive and may also have the advantage of time zone coverage. The UK and US are the largest client markets for LSO services. India is the largest offshore provider market.

---

* These figures only include LSO employees, not employees devoted to other service areas such as ITO or BPO.

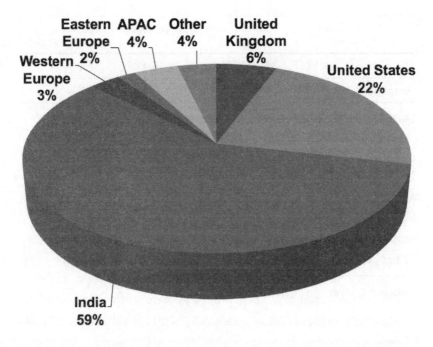

*Figure 2.4: LSPO Employment Headcount by Geographic Location*

We analysed the typical team composition overall, and the typical team composition for each service tower for 27 LSO providers (see Table 2.4). Across all service towers, the average team composition is 22 per cent onshore and 78 per cent offshore. The towers with the highest percentage of *onshore* resources are consulting and resourcing services. The towers with the highest percentage of *offshore* resources are employment and property services. As far as the range of team composition, one provider indicated that all their headcount is located onshore, while four LSO providers indicated that all their headcount is located offshore.

| | Sample size | Average % Onshore/Offshore |
|---|---|---|
| Litigation | 20 | 21%–79% |
| Intellectual property | 18 | 21%–79% |
| Corporate and compliance services | 15 | 20%–80% |
| Services procurement | 14 | 23%–77% |
| Employment services | 15 | 16%–84% |
| Property services | 14 | 18%–82% |
| Resources | 9 | 33%–67% |
| Consulting | 11 | 41%–59% |
| Overall Percentage | 23 | 22%–78% |

*Table 2.4: Average team composition*

Some LSO providers find it difficult to identify a 'typical' team composition. One LSO provider indicated, *'Currently, there is great variation across the solutions we have in place, always in response to client requirements. We are location-agnostic, meaning we have no preferred resource pool from which we draw.'*

## 2.9. LSO provider competencies

The 27 LSO providers were asked to assess their own competency for 186 processes across 22 services within the nine service towers using a scale from 0 to 3 based on the following definitions:

**Competency 0** indicates 'Our organisation does not provide this service'.

**Competency 1** indicates 'Our organisation can provide this service but it is not a core offering'.

**Competency 2** indicates 'Our organisation provides this service as a core offering'.

**Competency 3** indicates 'Our organisation excels at providing this service'.

To assess the maturity of the LSO market, we calculated the average competency score reported by LSO providers for the nine LSO service towers (see Figure 2.5). We only included LSO providers that choose to provide these services (i.e. providers who indicated a 0 across all processes within a service tower were excluded). Services procurement had the highest average competency score of 2.11 out of a possible 3.00. Property services had the lowest average competency score of 1.54. At least one LSO provider within each service tower reported that *'Our organisation excels at providing this service'* for all the processes within a service tower. Thus there are providers who consider their services quite mature within a service tower.

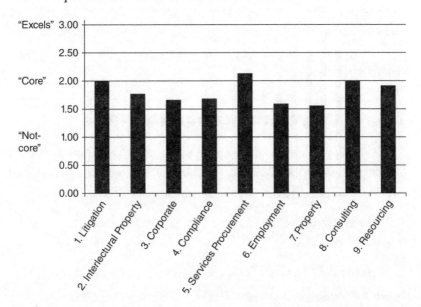

*Figure 2.5: Average LSO Self-Assessment by Service Tower*

Figure 2.6 shows a more detailed analysis, examining the average competency score reported by LSO providers for 22 specific services. We only included LSO providers that choose to provide these services (i.e. providers who indicated a 0 across all processes within a service were excluded). On average, the LSO service areas with the *most mature capabilities* are document management (n=24 out of 27 providers offer services in this space), contract management (n=26), services agreements (n=25), and transformational consulting (n=21). On average, the LSO service areas with the *least mature capabilities* are financing (n=12) and injury (n=16). For 19 of the 22 services, at least one LSO provider reported that they excel at all the processes within the service. Here, again, it becomes clear that clients will find at least some providers with mature capabilities for specific services.

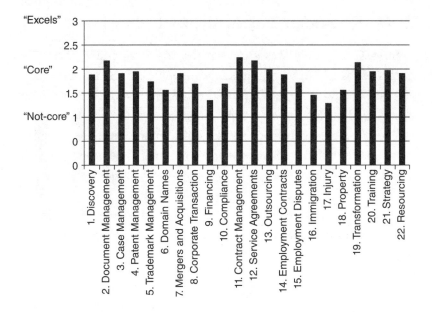

*Figure 2.6: Average LSO Self-Assessment by Service Tower*

Does size matter? We analysed whether a provider's competency for a service tower is related to the number of employees in that service tower. An analysis of variance indicates that a linear relationship is statistically significant (p = .0002) between headcount and competency (see Table 2.5). Size does matter: LSO providers with more employees, on average, report higher competencies than LSO providers with fewer employees.

| Competency: | Bottom quartile (Least competent) | Middle quartiles (Average competency) | Upper quartile (Most competent) |
|---|---|---|---|
| Average headcount | 11 | 45 | 104 |

*Table 2.5: Headcount and competency*

## 2.10. Provider capabilities model

From ITO and BPO research, we developed a model[4] that helps clients assess 12 important provider capabilities. These capabilities are certainly relevant to LSO provision. When evaluating providers, clients tend to focus on providers' resources because these are highly visible on site tours, balance sheets, and resumes. But they should be more interested in providers' ability to turn these resources – its physical and human assets such as physical facilities, technologies, tools and workforce – into capabilities that, in turn, can be combined to create high-level customer-facing competencies. Figure 2.7 illustrates the relationship between these three types of asset.

Outsourcing service companies need to demonstrate and utilise a mix of competencies:

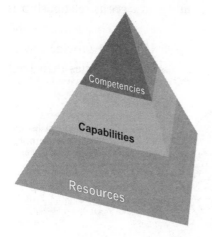

● *Delivery competency* sees the supplier providing a cost-effective, improved service performance against contractual terms and conditions and metrics (see Figure 2.8).

● *Transformation competency* is needed where a provider has agreed to deliver radically improved services in terms of cost, quality, and responsiveness (see Figure 2.9).

● *Relationship competency* is key. A client wants to engage the provider's capacity and expects the provider to align itself with the client's values, goals and needs to support long-term, critical business direction and change (see Figure 2.10).

*Figure 2.7: Resources, Capabilities, and Competencies*

The delivery competency is based on capabilities which determine the extent to which a provider can respond to a client's day-to-day operational services.

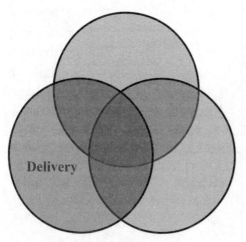

● Includes provider's domain expertise, business management capabilities, etc.

● Minimum requirement that clients seek in all providers.

● A provider's delivery competency – although crucial for success – may not serve to meaningfully distinguish providers.

*Figure 2.8: Delivery competency*

The transformation competency is based on capabilities which determine the extent to which a provider is equipped to delivery radically improved services in terms of cost, quality, and responsiveness.

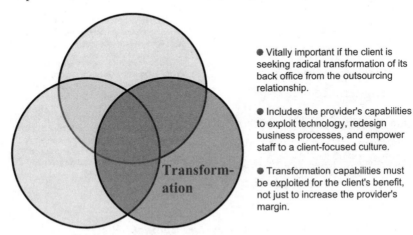

● Vitally important if the client is seeking radical transformation of its back office from the outsourcing relationship.

● Includes the provider's capabilities to exploit technology, redesign business processes, and empower staff to a client-focused culture.

● Transformation capabilities must be exploited for the client's benefit, not just to increase the provider's margin.

*Figure 2.9: Transformation competency*

The relationship competency is based on capabilities which determine the extent to which a provider is willing and able to align with the client's needs and goals.

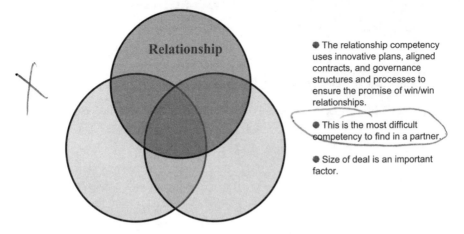

● The relationship competency uses innovative plans, aligned contracts, and governance structures and processes to ensure the promise of win/win relationships.

● This is the most difficult competency to find in a partner.

● Size of deal is an important factor.

*Figure 2.10: Relationship competency*

Clients tend to focus on the provider's delivery competency when they primarily want the provider to maintain or slightly improve existing services, such as maintaining legacy systems, operating data centres, or servicing a fleet of desktop devices in an ITO context. They tend to focus on the provider's transformation competency when they are seeking radical improvements in costs and services, but on the relationship competency when they are seeking a substantial and long-term commitment from the provider.

Our research demonstrates that managers have crucial roles to play in delivering 12 key provider capabilities that create the three competencies by relating to one another as shown in Figure 2.11.

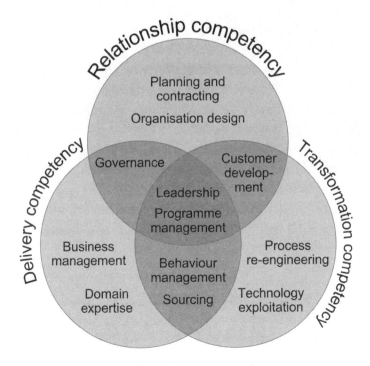

*Figure 2.11: Twelve capabilities providers need to develop*

Let us look at these capabilities and the related management and specialist tasks in more detail:

1. **Planning and contracting**: the provider's ability to design 'win/win' contracts that are flexible and responsive. Does the provider share with you its vision of the potential prize for both parties, and a coherent process for achieving it? Do they contract in ways that facilitate or contradict this process and prize? Does the contract inspire innovation through mandatory productivity improvement clauses, time allotted solely to drive the innovation agenda, and gainsharing mechanisms?[5]

2. **Account leadership**: the provider assigns an account lead who sets strategic direction with the client lead, aligns incentives, adapts to changes, motivates and inspires people, and delivers dramatic change. In practice, leadership is required at middle as well as top management levels because modern outsourcing is full of adaptive challenges requiring experiments, discoveries, adjustments and innovations from many different parts of the organisations involved. Look out for leaders only focused on meeting contractual service levels and margins. Check that the leader has strong relationships with the appropriate client-side leader, but also with the management of the provider's own organisation.

3. **Business management capability**: the provider's ability to deliver to service agreements and to the provider's and client's business plans. Clients often assume that providers must be good at this, and especially in driving out profit margins from their deals. But our own

research shows that, perennially, in at least 20 per cent of outsourcing arrangements, providers actually do not make money. This may be due to indifferent due diligence on their part in the face of understated costs of doing the work in-house as handed over by the client. Or the provider's sales people have staked everything on winning the bid, believing that margins can be achieved once the contract is signed, e.g. by additional work priced high because it is out of scope, or introducing high levels of automation. The problem for the client is that if business is bad for the provider, in time it becomes worse for the client as well, in the form of cost hikes and service degradation.

4. **Behaviour (people) management**: the provider's ability to hire, train, retain and inspire their employees to deliver high-level service. All major providers have employees to be proud of in terms of experience, skills, and knowledge. While clients tend to ask providers for proof of workforce quality such as resumes, average years of experience, turnover rate, and certifications, this will not serve to differentiate providers. Clients should also ask for evidence that the work force is empowered, satisfied, and customer-oriented. How do providers orient new employees to their culture? How do they reward and incent employee behaviour? In the LSO context, one client said that it was important for the client's operational people to visit the LSO provider's staff rather than just the client's senior leadership team. The operational people will be the ones working with the provider's staff and they will be able to assess provider employee competency and readiness.

5. **Domain expertise**: the provider's ability to apply professional knowledge for problem diagnosis, understanding and solutions. Look not just for technical know-how but for the much harder to acquire ability to understand the business, and experience in your specific kind of sectoral back-office environment, for example legal, procurement, IT, or human resources in a manufacturing environment. Providers need experience and knowledge not just of, for example, call centre work, but also of the industrial sector e.g. insurance, and the specific client organisation e.g. Allianz, Royal Insurance.

6. **Business re-engineering**: the provider's ability to incorporate changes to the service process to deliver dramatic improvements. The expertise involves designing and incorporating improvements to client processes and procedures. Check the provider's track record on re-engineering for clients, and also its skills and change capability.

7. **Technology exploitation**: the provider's ability to swiftly and effectively deploy technologies for business purposes. A major reason for the adoption of BPO and LSO is harnessing provider IT capability here, and getting them to make the IT investment you are reluctant to make. Is the capability available and are you contracting for its deployment, or just riding on a promise?

8. **Sourcing expertise**: the provider's ability to access and deploy resources cost-effectively as needed. Check out economies of scale claims, the availability of specialised professional skills you might need, and the dynamic

areas of quality and costs of staff in offshore locations. Also investigate claims of superior infrastructure and superior procurement practices.

9.  **Programme management**: the provider's ability to deliver a series of inter-related projects by managing change, transitions, upgrades and new solutions. This goes beyond project-level capabilities. Remember, you might want to expand your use of the provider, and the provider will have many other clients. These managers are invaluable in these circumstances. In our framework, the programme management capability occupies the central intersection of the relationship, delivery, and transformation competencies.

10. **Governance:** the provider's ability to define, track, take responsibility for and measure performance. In practice good governance has been found to make a big difference in outsourcing arrangements, so it is vital that the governance structures are well-designed and well-staffed. Governance structures including boards, operating committees, management meetings, escalation ladders and executive decision trees are essential to effective management of working processes and contractual agreements. However, by themselves they do not produce good performance – there are important follow-up questions. What reporting processes will be in place to ensure that each part of the governance structure is kept properly informed? What problem escalation procedures are defined? And what powers and sanctions are available through the governance structure?

11. **Organisational design**: the ability to design and implement successful organisational arrangements for relationship management. In practice providers vary greatly on their flexibility here. Some emphasise a 'thin' front end client team, interfacing with consolidated service units. This could constrain the ability to customise service and deliver to a specific client business plan. As a client, what degree of flexibility do you need? Our research found quite major deals sometimes taking two years to optimise client-provider organisation fit.

12. **Customer development**: the provider's ability to help turn 'users' into 'customers'. Whereas 'users' consume resources with little thought to costs, educated 'customers' make informed choices about service levels, functionality and costs they incur. The identification and negotiation of service levels and reporting on end-to-end service performance are important practices to aid the transformation from users to customers. We also found from our research that providers cannot create informed customers on their own; the client's retained organisation must be ready to shape the context for becoming a customer if meaningful change is to occur. Once complete, the shift from users to customers considerably empowers the client executives to more meaningfully contribute to business objectives. Rather than responding to a user's request with, 'I am sorry, it is not in my budget', the client executive works with the customer to consider the business value versus costs of customer requests.

In LSO do not expect your provider to have all these capabilities. In practice, depending on your requirements of course, you will probably **not** need all of them. If you want a straightforward improved service delivery at a competitive cost then the delivery competence is the one to focus on. If you want your provider to help you grow your business then the relationship competency becomes key. If you see your provider as a catalyst for significant change, check out its transformation competency, and the underpinning capabilities shown in Figure 2.11.

## 2.11. Conclusion

The 27 LSO providers analysed in this chapter provide a variety of services, including litigation, intellectual property, corporate, compliance, procurement, employment, property, and consulting services. We found that LSO providers allocated most of their human resources to litigation (26 per cent) and based most of their staff in India (59 per cent). We learned that LSO providers balance team composition to reduce client costs while still delivering quality services. We also gained insights into pricing and turnover.

We note, however, that the data on the 27 LSO providers do not represent a random sample, but rather a convenience sample. The disadvantage of a convenience sample is that it may include sampling bias, and thus may not represent the population of LSO providers. The advantages of this convenience sample are that we had access to a large amount of detailed data on services, prices, team composition, turnover, and more. Furthermore, considering the fierce competition in the LSO market, we think that prices are likely representative of the LSO provider population as of 2011. Another limitation is that provider competency relied on LSO provider self-assessment. Regardless of the limitations, the data does provide a broad look at the LSO provider landscape. We also know that the LSO provider landscape is not as mature as the broader BPO provider market, and the likelihood of any of the present LSO providers having all 12 capabilities indicated in Figure 2.11 is still low. Clients, therefore, should beware of provider claims on capabilities, and check their track record on actual delivery with previous clients through these assumed capabilities. The next chapter examines LSO from the client perspective.

1   Acharya, P. and Mahanty, P. (2007), 'Manpower shortage crisis in Indian information technology industry', *International Journal of Technology Management*, 38 (3); Kuruvilla, S. and Ranganathan, R. (2008), 'Economic development strategies and macro- and micro- level human resource policies: the case of Indian "outsourcing" industry', ILR Collection Articles and Chapters, Cornell University. http://digitalcommons.ilr.cornell.edu/articles/165 (accessed July 2013); Rai, S. (2005), 'Outsourcers struggling to keep workers in the fold', available at http://www.nytimes.com/2005/11/12/business/worldbusiness/12outsource.html (accessed July 2013).

2   Lacity, M., Iyer, V., and Rudramuniyaiah, P. (2008), 'Turnover Intentions of Indian IS Professionals', *Information Systems Frontiers*, Special Issue on Outsourcing of IT Services, Vol. 10, (2), pp. 225–41.

3   Luftman, J., and Ben-Zvi, T. (2011), 'Key Issues for IT Executives 2011: Cautious Optimism in Uncertain Times', *MIS Quarterly Executive*, Vol. 10, (4), pp. 203–12.

4   The model was first published in Feeny, D., Lacity, M., and Willcocks, L. (2005), 'Taking the Measure of Outsourcing Providers', *Sloan Management Review*, Vol. 46 (3) pp. 41–8.

5   Lacity, M. and Willcocks, L. (2013), 'Beyond Cost Savings: Outsourcing Business Processes for Innovation', *Sloan Management Review*, Vol. 54, (3) pp. 63–9.

# Chapter 3

# Client Perspectives: Recommended Practices

## 3.1. Introduction

In Chapter 2, we assessed LSO provider services, skill sets and qualifications, size of firm, geographic reach, pricing, team composition, staff turnover, and provider competencies for 27 LSO providers.[1] In this chapter, we seek to understand the practices that lead to good LSO performance. Based on in-depth interviews with clients and providers, we recommend a range of effective practices to ensure that LSO engagements meet client expectations. LSO 'clients' are in-house legal counsels or law firms.[2] The recommended 26 practices pertain to LSO strategy (3 practices), LSO provider selection (2 practices), stakeholder-buy-in (6 practices), contractual governance (3 practices), transition and co-ordination of work (7 practices), provider turnover (2 practices), relational governance (2 practices), and location of LSO staff (1 practice).

Our research method comprised five case studies based on interviews with client and provider representatives. Clients and providers were interviewed separately and all participants were guaranteed anonymity to promote open and frank discussions. We interviewed clients to appraise the performance of the LSO relationship and to understand the effectiveness of the practices client organisations used to decide, implement, and manage LSO engagements. Providers were asked similar questions to understand their perspectives on the same topics.

Table 3.1 provides an overview of the five LSO relationships. Each LSO relationship is assigned a Greek letter pseudonym ranging from Alpha to Epsilon. We use the convention of appending the Greek letter with the term 'Client' or 'Provider' to differentiate the client and provider firms, e.g. Alpha-Client connotes the client company and Alpha-Provider connotes the provider for the Alpha LSO relationship.

The five client companies are large, global companies, with revenues ranging between $2 billion and $74 billion; the average annual revenue is $39.6 billion. Employee headcount at the firm level range from 26,000 to over 200,000 employees; the average employee headcount is 103,786 people. The client executives interviewed held the titles of General Counsel (GC), Chief Counsel (CC), Manager, and Director. The client's enterprise legal functions range in size from 100 to 800 people. The five provider companies are all respected LSO firms, with an average employee headcount of 1,188 (range is 500 to 2,000 employees).[3] The provider executives we interviewed held titles of Chief Executive Officer (CEO), Senior Vice President (VP), Head, and Director.

Because our long-term research goal is to understand *best* LSO practices, the five relationships were chosen because they were identified by our research collaborator as high-performing LSO relationships. To validate that relationships were performing well, we asked each client, *'Overall, on a scale of 1 to 10, how would you rate the overall performance of the LSO relationship with a 1 indicating pitiful performance, a 5 indicating meets expectations overall, and a 10 indicating exceeds expectations?'* The clients gave responses ranging from 5 to 9, with an average response of 6.4. Even though all clients rated the LSO relationships as either meets or exceeds expectations on performance, all of the relationships experienced transition challenges and/or operational issues. As we learned, one practice that distinguishes performance is how the partners work together to resolve operational issues as they arise.

| LSO relationship | Contract start date | LSO provider headcount dedicated to the client | LSO delivery centre(s) serving client | Main LSO service(s) |
|---|---|---|---|---|
| Alpha | 2010 | About 18 lawyers | India | Broad set of services including compliance reporting, contract drafting, and contract database support. |
| Beta | 2009 | 12 to 18 lawyers | Primarily India; Some United States | Procurement support; research, document review, discovery, drafting, and compliance reporting. |
| Gamma | 2010 | 5 lawyers | Northern Ireland | Services procurement contract support. |
| Delta | 2010 | Varies widely from 24 to 120 lawyers depending on size of legal matter | Primarily India; Some United States | Document review for eDiscovery. |
| Epsilon | 2011 | 5 lawyers | Primarily India | Contract management. |

*Table 3.1: Overview of the LSO relationships*

## 3.2. Synopsis of the LSO case studies

In this section, we provide a synopsis for the five LSO relationships, including what prompted the client to consider LSO provision, the decision and selection process, and the performance outcomes thus far.

### Alpha-Client: Moving from captive centre to LSO provision

Alpha-Client is a large global firm with about 300 employees in its enterprise legal department. In 2007, Alpha-Client sought to reduce its legal spend. It decided to erect a captive centre in a low cost destination because a captive centre would serve to reduce legal costs while still retaining a high level of control. Alpha-Client chose India in 2008 because of its low costs and because the size of its legal labour pool is large. At its peak, the Indian captive centre employed 25 people, including lawyers, paralegals, and administrators. They performed tasks ranging from simple contract reviews and regulatory filings to administrative tasks like creating presentation materials. To manage the interface between the enterprise legal function and the captive centre, Alpha-Client assigned an expatriate manager to launch and manage the centre. Expatriates are expensive and difficult to recruit, and when the first one was re-assigned, a local manager took over. Soon after, the viability of the captive centre came into question because the turnover rate was 40 per cent and the captive centre needed a significant financial investment in tools and technologies to better manage workflow – money Alpha-Client did not want to spend.

Alpha-Client decided to look for an LSO provider to buy the captive centre. The GC assembled a team to manage the tendering process, which was guided significantly by Alpha-Client's procurement department to ensure compliance around policies like ethical sourcing.

The team narrowed the selection to two LSO providers. Alpha-Provider was selected ultimately because of its strengths in people, processes, and technologies and because of its experience with serving large Western-based clients. In addition, Alpha-Client's GC said, *'They were flexible on the terms and conditions and their pricing was keen as well. They had a creative lead...I think he was impressive.'* Overall, Alpha-Client reports that the LSO provider is meeting expectations because the cost savings are significant and because the GC has been able to keep internal headcount flat, despite increased workload.

## Beta-Client: Using LSO to reduce costs and to refocus in-house legal staff

Beta-Client is a large global firm with about 100 employees in its enterprise legal function. Year-on-year, the enterprise legal function was experiencing rising legal fees from their external law firms. The Global Financial Crisis (GFC) of 2008 was the catalyst that required all of Beta-Client's back office functions – including legal – to reduce costs, and outsourcing was seen as a key strategy for accomplishing cost reduction. A small team within the enterprise legal function was charged with looking at outsourcing as a way to reduce external legal fees and to focus in-house lawyers on more value-added tasks. The team's idea was to use an LSO provider for tasks assigned typically to junior lawyers, such as research, document review, discovery, drafting, contract review and compliance reporting. Beta-Client's CC said, *'The specific objectives around the decision were really two-fold. The primary one was around cost reduction. The other one was freeing up our in-house lawyers from some of the less complex work they have on their desk so they could be focusing on the more strategic type of work, be it a bit more customer facing.'* Beta-Client committed to outsourcing in April 2009. With input from procurement, the team issued a Request for Proposal (RFP) and narrowed the selection to four LSO providers. Beta-Provider was selected based on costs, time zone compatibility, resource scalability, and proven ability to service Western Clients. The contract is based on a fixed-fee pricing structure for a number of Full Time Equivalents (FTEs) (varying from 12 to 18).

Beta-Client reports that the LSO relationship is meeting cost and quality expectations. Pertaining to costs, Beta-Client has saved millions in legal fees each year. The Chief Counsel (CC) added, *'Instead of paying say $250 and $300 per hour for a junior lawyer in a law firm, we are using LSO resources. We've seen significant savings on projects around that.'*

### Gamma-Client: Including an LSO on a select legal panel

Gamma-Client is the largest firm in our sample. At Gamma-Client, the General Counsel (GC) decided in 2010 to reduce the number of law firm partners by conducting a panel review: *'The reason that we wanted to put a legal panel together was that we were using over 70 law firms simply in connection with our corporate headquarters, which is an awful lot of people to have relationships with. I wanted to have closer, deeper, longer-term relationships with fewer law firms.'* The GC wanted to include an LSO provider on its final panel: *'I was quite keen to look at the possibility of having an alternative legal service provider on our panel to keep the law firms on their toes.'* Gamma-Client considered four LSO providers. Two offshore specialty LSO providers were eliminated because Gamma-Client did not have enough volume of work to send to the LSO providers. One domestic LSO provider was eliminated because costs were too high. Gamma-Client selected a large global LSO provider which they already had a relationship with for secondment services. Gamma-Provider set up a delivery centre in Northern Ireland with a dedicated team of five lawyers to service Gamma-Client. Although the dedicated team is small, the team supports 40 different procurement categories spanning 45 countries.

At Gamma-Client, the GC selected services procurement as the legal work to source through Gamma-Provider. Services procurement work comprises many small-valued contracts which can be largely standardised. The GM said, *'Services procurement looked like it was going to be a relatively easy area of work to say, "This is how we do it" and to commoditise it as far as possible. Services procurement felt like the right place to start because there are a lot of small value contracts that get drawn up in that area of work. So, it was low value/high volume, classic LSO stuff.'*

Gamma-Client's GC is pleased with the cost savings of about 30 per cent and praised Gamma-Provider's ability to deliver on their service level agreements: *'They do quite well on meeting the SLA requirement on transactional matters and our internal customers and colleagues love them to bits! They are fantastic and good for us because it gives us a halo effect.'* In addition to cost savings delivered, Gamma-Client reports that the LSO service provider delivers innovations in the areas of measurement and reporting.

## Delta-Client: Using LSO for scalability and cost reduction

Delta-Client's enterprise legal department employs about 800 people. About four years ago, the litigation department re-designed its processes, quality control, and its relationships with external legal firms. In particular, Delta-Client wanted more control over document review pertaining to legal matters rather than just delegating that task to its external legal firms, which was quite expensive. In 2010, Delta-Client was dealing with a large legal matter that would require reviewing millions of documents. It convinced its UK-based external law firm to work together to engage an LSO provider for this work. The UK-law firm questioned whether documents reviewed outside the UK would be admissible in UK courts, but Delta-Client worked with the UK courts to confirm that the practice was acceptable. Delta-

Client worked closely with the UK law firm during the LSO provider selection. After a Request For Information (RFI), two LSO providers were selected for a competitive pilot project (the pilot is explained in more detail in the LSO provider selection section of this report). After Delta-Provider won the competition, it was hired to review documents for a large legal matter. The team estimated that Delta-Provider would need about 50 lawyers to do the document review, but the partners quickly realised they needed closer to 120 lawyers. Delta-Provider astonished its client by ramping up with qualified lawyers within a month. After this project, the partners signed an opened-ended, long-term Master Service Agreement based on hourly rates.

Delta-Client is very pleased with the LSO relationship, because of its lower costs, work quality, and most importantly – scalability. Delta-Client reports total overall savings of about 40 per cent compared to doing work onshore. Pertaining to work quality, the Director said, *'They have some pretty high QC standards...like 97 per cent accuracy...'* On the value of scalability, Delta-Client's Director said, *'If you look at eDiscovery and document review in particular, the volume of work is so spiky. I am very happy for Delta-Provider to manage that risk and be able to staff up and ramp down.'*

## Epsilon-Client: Guaranteeing quality on repetitive work

Epsilon-Client is unique among the relationships in that the LSO decision was championed from within a Business Services organisation rather than within the enterprise legal function. Business Services is responsible for support functions including human resources, finance, procurement, and information systems.

Epsilon-Client was concerned about the risk exposure of how their contracts related to intellectual property across all their regions, so they created a centralised process that would require all contracts to be tagged with multiple attributes. The backlog of existing contracts was huge, so Epsilon-Client hired a BPO to tag more than 200,000 contracts. That engagement went well. Epsilon-Client realised that going forward, the tagging of new contracts and management of existing contracts would involve a lot of repetitive work. By assigning contract management work to an LSO, the legal department could assign in-house lawyers more strategic work. A manager from Epsilon-Client said, *'The main driver was never to save costs. The driver was, "Are we able to free up our people to focus on different stuff?" and also, even more important: "Are we able to guarantee a consistent quality?"'*.

Epsilon-Client issued an RFP and invited both BPO and LSO providers to respond. It selected Epsilon-Provider partly because it had an existing relationship with Epsilon-Provider's parent organisation. Epsilon-Client expected synergies from having a bundled relationship. The client representative thinks this was a good choice, as the partners have never had a major conflict and the quality of work has been very high.

## 3.3. **LSO strategy**

*'We are transitioning our own legal team from bedside doctors to people who are trying to get the process to move as fast as it possibly can.'* – General Counsel

According to management guru Alfred D. Chandler[4], *strategy* is the determination of the basic long-term goals and objectives of an enterprise, and the adoption of courses of action and the allocation of resources necessary for carrying out these goals. LSO clients must decide how LSO fits into a larger picture of transforming legal services and learn to disaggregate legal work to achieve 'best sourcing'. Clients should also consider the possible value of LSO provision besides cost savings. The following practices pertaining to strategy are recommended.

## Practice 1: Conceive of LSO in the context of a larger transformation of legal services

As a strategy, LSO is best conceived as a part of a larger transformation of legal services.[5] For a long time, the legal profession has recognised that its primary business model – charging clients by the hour – does not align incentives well. Under this model, law firms are actually incentivised to spend as much time as possible on a client's legal issue. One GC explained, '*I have a problem with the entire business model of charging by the hour because it seems to me the more hours you can charge the more money you can make for the business. And, when you're a client, you actually want your lawyers to spend the least possible time on your issues, because you don't want these issues to grow out of proportion.*' External law firms also have a culture of always delivering *quality*, but not necessarily *value*. As one GC said, '*Law firms struggle with doing anything other than a Porsche or Rolls Royce level of service and they're not quite happy with a dodgy Buick, which is all that I might need.*'

Enterprise legal functions and law firms need increasingly to think about best sourcing – packaging legal work and assigning it to the most efficient and effective source, whether the source is in-house lawyers, captive LSO centres, or LSO providers. Work should be pushed to the most effective deliverer.

## Practice 2: Move towards the digital assembly line by disaggregating work

Best sourcing legal work requires enterprise legal functions and law firms to disaggregate legal work. Rather than assigning a legal matter entirely to one source such as an external law firm, for example, the work could be broken down to multiple tasks and work assigned to different sources. For example, Mergers and Acquisitions (M&A) is not high volume for most enterprise functions, but within M&A some tasks have a lot of volume that could be sourced by an LSO provider.

The CEO for one provider in our study compared the evolution of the legal profession to the evolution in the medical profession. Medicine has evolved away from the family doctor who performs all medical services to trained specialists. He said: *'In the old days you went to a doctor for everything. I remember growing up in India, the doctor even had a compounder and would prepare all the medicines and give it to you right there. Today, medicine is all unbundled services. Today, you go to a doctor, he sends you to a specialist, the specialist sends you to a technician to take your x-ray. You have technicians and nurse practitioners who are specialists, but they are not doctors. I think the legal profession is headed this way too. People are starting to look at legal services in a systems, process-oriented manner because technology and globalisation allow you to do that.'*

Other providers in our study, however, have a different view on disaggregation by objecting to the idea that LSO providers will only perform carved-out, low-level tasks. One provider, for example, said if only low level tasks are outsourced, then maybe five or 10 percent of work can be transformed. He conjectured: *'If an entire set of legal work is outsourced, then real transformation becomes possible.'*

## Practice 3: Consider LSO provision for more than just cost savings

As we noted in Chapter 1, clients are initially attracted to LSO because of the potential for cost savings. Indeed, the clients we interviewed use LSO providers to reduce costs by 30 per cent to 50 per cent. But the clients also sought and realised additional value from LSO services, including the ability to focus in-house legal staff on higher-value work, scalability, and to improve quality.

**Focus in-house lawyers on more strategic work.** In our study, none of the clients were using LSO to cut in-house legal staff. To the contrary, the GCs from the client companies wanted their in-house lawyers to focus on more value-added and more interesting work. One GC represents all the clients in our study when he said, *'We are doing this because there are a whole bunch of tasks that are just being done inefficiently by the team.'* He told his in-house lawyers: *'Here's an opportunity for you to stop doing those tasks and to focus on more value-added stuff, which is what every General Counsel I have spoken to has put into place.'*

**Enhance scalability.** Scalability can be improved by hiring an LSO provider to meet short term increases in demand. One client, for example, uses an LSO provider to help with large document reviews. The LSO provider astonished its client by ramping up with 150 qualified lawyers within a month's notice.

**Improve quality.** Many clients may assume that an LSO provider's quality will be lower than work performed by in-house staff. With LSO, however, work products are more rigorously tracked and some clients report that quality improved with outsourcing. One client said, *'With internal people, you rarely check their work product on quality or at least you don't check it as frequently or in as much detail as you do your supplier. We had data quality and I knew at one point it was around 40 per cent, but now we have a data quality of 99.8 per cent with our LSO provider. So, it's a huge difference.'*

**Add value.** Although cost reduction, the ability to focus in-house legal staff on higher-value work, scalability, and to improve quality are the client business objectives that emerged from the LSO case studies, clients might leverage LSO for additional value such as speed of delivery, utility pricing, to spur competition, process transformation, access to innovation (particularly IT-enabled innovations), access to new markets, and setting up an LSO business with a provider (see Chapter 1).

## 3.4. **LSO provider selection**

*'We selected our provider because of their flexibility and their willingness to do what is right for us.'* – Client Director

The clients in our sample went through the usual outsourcing procurement process by issuing RFIs or RFPs to narrow the selection and then assessing more thoroughly the short-listed providers. All the clients in our sample assembled decision teams that included people from the enterprise legal function and from the procurement department, the latter whose role was to ensure compliance with the company's sourcing policies. Two practices pertaining to LSO provider selection emerged from the interviews:

### Practice 4: Consider overall value and provider capabilities, not just price

As noted in the strategy section, clients adopt LSO to significantly reduce costs, but clients should not select an LSO provider based solely on price. Clients should assess providers on a number of capabilities, including those described in the previous chapter.

The clients we interviewed selected providers based on prices, quality of work, turnaround times, flexibility, and proven track records. One client, for example, worked with procurement to develop the RFP, but the GC crafted the selection process to make sure the least expensive provider did not become the automatic winner. He wanted a provider that had great processes, technologies, and people in addition to lower costs. Another CC selected his LSO provider based on costs, time zone compatibility, resource scalability, and proven ability to service Western clients.

### Practice 5: Test provider capabilities with a controlled experiment

If a client plans to engage an LSO provider for a significant volume of work, they might consider testing provider capabilities with a controlled experiment like one client in our study. The client has the largest LSO engagement amongst those we studied, which fluctuates in size from 24 to 120 Full Time Equivalents (FTEs). Because the account was going to be large, the client wanted a better way to assess provider capabilities than merely going through the normal procurement process. The client used an RFI to narrow the selection to two providers, and then it organised a controlled experiment by assigning the two LSO providers and an external legal firm to review the same set of documents (nearly 20,000 of them) within a two week period. The external legal firm – the client's strategic, long-term partner – served as the benchmark. The client scored providers on 20 criteria. The competing teams knew how their work would be evaluated. The experiment was expensive, but the client was confident it helped to fully test provider capabilities.

## 3.5. Contractual governance

*'We have a fixed per person rate for a dedicated team and then with project teams there is a mix of hourly and day rates.'* – Chief Counsel

Contractual governance is the formal, written contractual agreement between the LSO client and provider. Compared to the level of contract maturity in ITO and BPO contracts,[6] we did not find the same level of contract maturity for LSO contracts, particularly for pricing and Service Level Agreements (SLAs). All of the LSO relationships we studied have some type of SLA as part of the Master Service Agreement (MSA) or as part of specific Statements of Work (SOW), but SLAs were typically limited to the quality and/or timeliness of work and spot checks on client satisfaction. Some clients also receive reports on the provider's efficiency, however, the measures and reporting mechanisms varied among our sample. Despite the lack of maturity on many accounts, clients were generally satisfied with their LSO contractual governance mechanisms.

## Practice 6: Use fixed-fee FTE pricing for cost predictability, simplicity, and ease of administration

Most of the LSO relationships we studied use a fixed-fee pricing structure for a specified number of FTEs. One contract, for example, has fixed fees for junior lawyers and a higher fixed fee for senior people. Another client's contract is fixed-fee for the dedicated team and a mix of hourly and day rates for special project teams.

Clients like the predictability, simplicity, and ease of administration of this pricing mechanism. Clients easily estimate cost savings by comparing LSO rates with in-house or legal firm rates, with some adjustment for productivity. For example, one client estimates the time it takes an in-house lawyer to do a task compared to an offshore LSO lawyer for a sample of projects. The LSO lawyers are not (yet) as productive as in-house lawyers, but the costs are so much cheaper offshore, that total costs are still significantly lower offshore than onshore, even with lower offshore productivity rates factored into the assessment.

For FTE-priced deals we studied, contracts include service levels for quality, turnaround time, and client satisfaction. The LSO clients primarily rely on spot assessments of client satisfaction. At one client's company, for example, its internal lawyers fill in a customer satisfaction form after the completion of a major project. If the score is ever below the agreed-upon level, the partners immediately address the issue. Another client has a number of SLAs covering turnaround time, unnecessary escalation (i.e. the provider escalated a question or issue back to the client that was unnecessary), quality, and customer satisfaction. Customer satisfaction is measured at the completion of every significant negotiation. The provider also has 15 per cent of their fees at risk for non-performance, but the clause has never been triggered.

Overall, the clients we interviewed are generally satisfied with the fixed-fee FTE pricing mechanism. For example, one CC said, '*We have been pretty happy with it so far; we haven't looked to tweak that in any way.*' According to the clients we interviewed, FTE pricing has better incentives than the hourly rate model because the LSO providers have to be efficient to meet their service level agreements. One GC described FTE pricing as a change in mindset. LSO providers have to think: '*How can we maximise the throughput so I can meet the service level agreement?*' rather than: '*How many hours can I charge the client for?*'

### Practice 7: Use unit pricing if work is standardised and volume is large

In ITO and BPO, many contracts have unit prices, such as price per user supported, price per invoice processed, and price per policy administered. The advantage of unit pricing is that clients pay for volume of output rather than volume of input, such as hours worked. In the LSO context, only one client originally used unit pricing but neither the client nor its provider was satisfied with the unit pricing mechanism. The partners assumed that work would be so repetitive that the work could be allocated to any of the provider's slack resources. Without a dedicated team, however, response times to queries were slow and none of the provider's employees built up client-specific expertise. The partners renegotiated and moved to FTE pricing, with five provider employees devoted to the account.

Other clients we interviewed said that pricing per unit is difficult because the volume of services is not as high in legal functions compared to other back office functions. For example, finance and accounting may process millions of invoices and can calculate an average price per invoice processed. One GC said, *'We haven't linked price at any specific volume criteria at this point.'* As another GC said, *'I think one of the challenges of unit pricing is finding enough volume to get to that kind of model. Legal services have much less volume altogether.'* In the future, however, this GC foresees that pricing models can evolve in LSO, such as pricing per contract.

LSO providers seem more ready than LSO clients to move to transaction-based pricing. One LSO provider, for example, describes their output-based pricing, *'We rarely use resource-based pricing (hourly, daily, weekly or otherwise). Instead, we prefer to use output-based pricing because it better aligns incentives between [LSO provider] and its clients. Billing on a time and materials basis penalises the provider for investing in efficiency and productivity, which would reduce the amount of billable time. As we view our ability to deliver efficiency and productivity gains as a core strength, we prefer to bill on an output-based model that rewards us for productivity gains while passing on most of the gains to clients in the form of lower cost per unit of work.'*

LSO clients might also consider a number of service level agreements that are standard or emerging in ITO and BPO contracts.[7] Here are three that encourage providers to improve performance over time.

## Practice 8: Mandate yearly productivity improvements

Although clients like the simplicity and predictability of FTE pricing, many clients also realise that input-based pricing discourages the provider from implementing innovations that would reduce the number of FTEs because the provider's revenues would decrease. To overcome this disincentive, many ITO/BPO clients necessitate innovation by mandating productivity improvement requirements in the contract that require the provider to improve the client's productivity, most typically by four to five per cent per year. Both clients and providers reported positive results from mandatory productivity targets.

## Practice 9: Dedicate time each year to drive the innovation agenda

ITO and BPO clients often expect their providers to be constantly innovating by introducing new methods, tools, and technologies. Innovation objectives can quickly slide down the list of priorities if everyone's attention is focused on operations. In high-performing ITO/BPO contracts, the partners don't let operational issues stall innovation; they contractually dedicate time each year to drive the innovation agenda. The client and provider typically identify four to six innovation projects for the coming year and agree how those projects would be funded. They also use the next practice to agree on how the benefits should be allocated.

## Practice 10: Gainshare the benefits from specific innovation projects

Among all the ways to promote innovation, gainsharing packs the most punch because it promises to increase the provider's revenue as well as the client's performance. On an innovation survey, 79 per cent of clients, 77 per cent of providers, and 78 per cent of advisers indicated that gainsharing on innovation benefits was the best way to promote innovation.[8] However, in a follow-up question, clients indicated that only 40 per cent of innovations delivered on their accounts used gainsharing. Paired interviews with BPO clients and providers also found fewer than half the clients contracting for gainsharing clauses, or even when gainsharing was included in the contract, only half of these clients availed the gainsharing option. On the other hand, a quarter of clients interviewed reported that gainsharing was prompting powerful innovations on their accounts. What distinguished successful from unsuccessful gainsharing? Gainsharing was most effective when used at the project level. Clients and providers who built a business case for each innovation project and agreed in advance how the financial compensation would be allocated, reported great results with gainsharing.

## 3.6. Stakeholder buy-in

*'Lawyers think they are important, but it's just another service'* – General Counsel

Engaging an LSO provider, particularly for the first time, represents a radical shift in the sourcing of legal work. Proponents of the LSO relationship are the stakeholders who will 'gain' the most benefits from it, such as GCs held responsible for corporate legal spend. The clients we interviewed also reported that c-suite executives and business unit heads were supportive or at least accustomed to outsourcing, as many of these client companies have existing outsourcing contracts for information technology, finance, accounting, human resources, and customer support services. These stakeholders accept and expect the targeted outsourcing of legal services.

Opponents to legal outsourcing are the stakeholders who *think* they have the most to lose – the in-house lawyers and the external legal firms were the most resistant stakeholders. Many lawyers think along the lines of, *'We are part of the mystical craft of specialists. We're professionals, and you can't commoditise us'* said one GC. *'The main concern was that the LPO provider would not be capable of doing the work,'* said another client. The in-house legal teams were generally more accepting of outsourcing parts of discovery and less accepting of outsourcing parts of due diligence, because discovery work is seen as less specialised. Another GC said of his internal lawyers, *'Certainly within our in-house team the sceptics think that LSO was irrelevant because the level of complexity of the work they had was not suitable to provide to the LSO.'* To get in-house lawyers on board, the following practices were suggested:

## Practice 11: Communicate early and involve in-house lawyers

As previously noted, none of the client firms we interviewed intended to use LSO providers to replace in-house lawyers. To the contrary, the GCs from the client companies wanted their in-house lawyers to focus on more value-added and more interesting work. In addition to assuring in-house lawyers that LSO was not replacing them, the GCs had to convince them that LSO would make their jobs easier and more interesting; they needed to hear this reasoning early and often.

Not all internal lawyers will have the time or inclination to be involved in the LSO decision process. But having representatives from among the legal staff will facilitate buy-in and can lead to better decisions. One CG said, *'In starting the LPO, we got the lawyers who would be working with them and whose work would be impacted by them, involved early on so they would be part of building the future; communicating with our own people to enable them to understand why we were doing it and to get them into a position where they too wanted it to be a success rather than them feeling threatened by it or wanting it to fail.'*

## Practice 12: Prove the Concept

In-house lawyers legitimately question whether an LSO provider is capable of doing their work. One Manager from a client company said that he tested LSO with a low-risk, three-month pilot project. He measured the quality of work for every work product coming out of India. He said, *'After three months, they saw that the quality was so high that they were convinced that these people were very good. That really impressed them.'* Our prior research on ITO and BPO also found that pilot projects test the outsourcing concept and allow clients to quickly learn from mistakes before engaging in a longer term contract. Some providers, however, may not respond to an RFP for a small pilot project because the transaction costs are high for providers and the profits are low.[9] Providers need to be convinced that the pilot will likely lead to a more substantial relationship.

## Practice 13: Use Key Performance Indicators to incentivise adoption by in-house lawyers

In-house lawyers find it easier to pass work off to an external law firm than to an LSO provider because the external law firms will know how to perform the work with little instruction. Therefore, in-house lawyers have to be encouraged to use the LSO provider. Key Performance Indicators can motivate in-house lawyers to adopt LSO provision. At one client, the CC has an internal KPI that requires his team to become more efficient each year, which essentially functions as a directive to use the LSO provider. The CC said, *'We have sort of an internal mandate to use our LSO provider which is reflected in our performance requirements, our performance KPIs, if you like...I think it is truly important that each of your in-house lawyers have a personal objective around what they need to get out of the LSO arrangement. Pulling some of those levers is important to overcome any resistance.'*

### Practice 14: Invest in face-to-face meetings

One practice to overcome resistance is for everyone to meet face-to-face. At one client company, a senior leader visits India every six months. The GC said, *'It does add to the expense but we thought it was worthwhile.'* Face-to-face meetings have additional benefits, such as building group cohesion. One client said that his team visited the LSO staff in India and that they built a close rapport with the employees. The client's Director explained, *'What I found in talking with the management afterwards, is that really went a long way in just getting them to know our company, getting to know our people, and knowing that we care about the project and that it was important to us versus them being some factory where people are sending them stuff and expecting it to come back. I didn't realise that it had that impact, but I'm glad it did.'* Another client advised that if you can only afford to send one or two people to India, send operations people who can transfer knowledge to the provider's staff. If only senior executives from the client organisation visit the provider then, as the client says, *'You sit around, drink coffee, and show each other how great you are.'*

## 3.7. Transition and co-ordination of work

*'If you think you can just throw the work over the fence and expect to get something back exactly as you like without any other investment, chances are they will not be that successful on their own.'* – Chief Counsel

The clients we interviewed reported different levels of success during the transition of work to the LSO provider. The client who reported the easiest transition relied on the more experienced provider to drive the transition process. The Director explained: *'Our provider does a very good job of transition…[they] walked us through the whole process.'* Others had rockier transitions, but all participants learned that the transition and co-ordination of work requires the right leadership, documentation, communication, and processes. The following practices were recommended:

## Practice 15: Assign a high-level point person to manage the LSO provider relationship

Clients in our study have a client lead in charge of the LSO relationship. This person should have experience, personal credibility and political clout within the client organisation, which normally requires a senior person, most typically a direct report to the GC. Providers all appreciate the value of a supportive high-level point person. For example, the VP of one provider said of his client's point person, *'His job is to make sure that elements that need to be engaged from the client side are engaged. We talk every week and have on-site meetings once every other quarter. That kind of relationship has been very, very crucial in making this relationship a success, in addition to the executive sponsorship.'* The Head of Managed Services for another provider said that his team leads meet with the client lead every week to go through prioritisation, questions of legal substance, and to address any issues. They also talk about the team, team members, travel schedules, training schedules, and the pipeline of work. The provider said, *'There's lots of open sharing.'*

## Practice 16: For larger projects or engagements, use an onshore engagement manager (OEM)

An Onshore Engagement Manager (OEM) is employed by the LSO provider but works at or near to the client site to co-ordinate work. Because the OEM is familiar with both the client's and LSO provider's processes, technologies, cultures, and employees, the OEM smoothes the transitions of work between the client and LSO provider. The

OEMs also take the burden of manning late night conference calls, clarifying client requirements, and addressing time zone bottlenecks if the provider is located offshore. Because of the expense of an OEM, the practice is best suited for project work, such as a large legal matter, where playbooks cannot be defined fully in advance and when requirements emerge as the legal matter progresses. One client, for example, assigns an onshore project manager to work directly with the client's project manager. The Director explains the value of the OEM: *'And the good thing there is I have somebody I can call during the day or my outside counsel has someone they can call during their business day to say, "Hey, here is the issue we are seeing" or "Here are some things we want you to deal with." And that person is responsible for being up in the middle of the night to make sure they are feeding the information to the team in India. So we've always got somebody in our time zone to deal with.'* The client trained the OEM along with its own legal team to transfer as much knowledge as possible. The idea is that the OEM is qualified to step in to be the client's discovery project manager. The Director explained the dual purpose for training the OEM: *'One, it would help them better understand our organisation, our process, and how we do things. Two, it gives me some overflow capacity. If my team were to get too busy, we could bring this person in and have him just do our job.'*

## Practice 17: Build a playbook to specify requirements

Playbooks and other supporting documents like process maps and checklists provide instructions to the LSO provider's team. The clients report that LSO providers are quite good at developing and updating playbooks. A VP for one provider explained, *'We create a checklist, playbooks, guidelines, process maps and all the other things that go into making a focused quality programme. Every work request is treated with the same quality of standards that we agree that they will follow.'* The playbooks and other supporting documents help lawyers trained in one country (like India) to understand the nuances and legal requirements of serving clients from other countries (like the United States). Playbooks also standardise service and establish clear lines of responsibility. The Director for one client explained that playbooks '...*provided us with the understanding of how to better manage all of our document reviews. Things like the quality control checks, the communications, the standing meetings, those kinds of things. Having that template to kind of get things going really seems to help out a lot.'*

Playbooks, however, must be used wisely. One client warned that the provider executed exactly from the playbook and never proactively sought to improve it. The client said, *'What they didn't do is come back and say, "This is unclear and we have to change this in order to make the process run more smoothly." They just followed the process until we said, "Guys, this is just wrong", and then we adapted the playbook.'*

## Practice 18: Build a portal to direct work to the best source

Portals serve as 'front doors' for people within a firm to request legal services. Portals require people to specify consistently the type, scope, requirements, and timing of legal work and can be used to route work to the best source. One GC wanted to relieve his legal staff from performing all the small tasks colleagues ask specific lawyers to perform as a 'favour'. All requests for legal services now go through a portal that has rules for directing requests by type to the best legal source. The GC said, *'The portal sources to the right people. For some particular types of work, my team doesn't even see the request because it automatically goes to [the provider].'*

### Practice 19: Direct in-house lawyers to nurture the LSO provider's lawyers

Many lawyers expect that an LSO provider should have the same level of experience and produce the same quality of work as lawyers from an external law firm. Such expectations are unrealistic, and may result in a negative perception of the LSO provider's performance. One GC said, '*That's a challenge to overcome that people still think of them as external lawyers. They have a bad experience and they think they are not going back to the LPO provider rather than ask, "How do I get them up to speed so they don't do that again?"* The GC asked his internal lawyers to think of the LSO's staff as part of their junior team that needs mentoring. He asked them to chat with them, invest time in getting to know them, and help them to be successful.

### Practice 20: Have joint and frequent communications with the client, external legal counsel, the LSO provider and, if relevant, the technology provider

All the clients we interviewed stressed the importance of frequent communications between the client and LSO provider. One CC, for example, said, '*Good and frequent communications are certainly key.*' Planned meetings may be scheduled daily or weekly depending on the type of work assigned to the provider. The co-ordination of work, however, often entails other stakeholders besides the client and LSO provider. At one client company, having all parties on weekly calls was one of the key lessons learned. When the LSO provider is given conflicting instructions from the client and external law firm, a tri-way call was the best way to resolve it, or a four-way call if the tool from the technology provider was involved.

## Practice 21: Learn from other in-house functions that have outsourced services

Our LSO research uncovered the same cultural issues found in ITO and BPO research.[10] For example, many Indians did not ask for instructions to be clarified if they didn't understand the client fully. Instead, Indian teams often 'took their best shot' and then found out they completely misunderstood the client's requirements. The LSO clients we interviewed said that they had to create a culture that rewarded and welcomed when the Indian team asked questions, pushed back, and challenged the client. One GC commented, *'So, giving them the courage to go and clarify their instructions was certainly something that took a little entrenching in the beginning. Giving them confidence to go back and clarify their instructions and so on. That's certainly been one of the things that we've been doing over the initial year.'*

The LSO client champion who worked in his company's Business Services organisation actually brought a tremendous amount of learning to LSO from his personal relationships and from his company's existing ITO and BPO relationships. He said his company doesn't repeat mistakes learned from outsourcing IT and finance. For example, he has long known that procuring services cannot be about getting a low-cost provider because quality will suffer. He said, *'You get what you pay for'* and added, *'Don't expect you can move the mess you have internally to someone else and it will get sorted out.'*

Although this is the first time the client firms in this study outsourced legal services, it is not the first time their firms have outsourced business services. Seasoned client executives from other support functions like IT, HR, and Finance had already conquered the outsourcing learning curve of packaging work, designing process interfaces, and bridging cultural differences. In hindsight, some of the clients we interviewed wished they would have sought the advice from other functional areas. For example, one client said, *'I wish we could have spent a little more time working with somebody in our business group that was familiar with outsourcing.'*

## 3.8. Provider turnover

*'Turnover has been very, very low. It has had absolutely no impact at all to me.'* – one LSO client

*'The turnover has been high within the dedicated team.'* – another LSO client

High staff turnover in low-cost countries has been a major problem for ITO, BPO, and LSO providers. In India, LSO turnover rates in Gurgaon can be as high as 30 per cent because the proliferation of providers makes it easy for workers to find alternative employment. Other Indian cities have LSO turnover rates between 8 per cent and 10 per cent. Clients and providers understand that turnover will occur. The GC for one client said, *'Turnover is a reality of outsourcing. It is a challenge because, obviously, some of the more talented lawyers over a period of time look for their next move. So, you need to have good systems in place on their part so that capturing knowledge and sharing that knowledge is within team.'* The following practices can protect clients from the adverse effects of attrition:

### Practice 22. Have the LSO provider overstaff the project to mitigate turnover risks

Transitioning work to an LSO provider requires a significant amount of knowledge transfer upfront. Clients only want to do this expensive and time-consuming training once. Given that provider staff will experience turnover – either unwanted turnover from resignations or wanted turnover from poor employee performance – one client suggested that providers overstaff at the beginning of a project. Given that rates are so much cheaper with LSO, the extra headcount will not severely erode the business case. One client explained, *'Typically, the provider overstaffs the team initially in case they need to weed out some people... So if we need 20 people, maybe we will put 25 people through the initial training.'*

## Practice 23: Keep playbooks updated to protect against turnover effects

Playbooks and other process documents are valuable not only for transitioning and co-ordinating work, but for mitigating the effects of LSO employee turnover. Detailed playbooks that are frequently updated will bring new employees up to speed quickly. One GC explained, *'You developed a playbook so that even if the individual who's been working on this particular area goes, the impact would be reduced because all that knowledge and issues and understanding are being caught and you're always upgrading.'* The VP from a provider added that the playbooks, processes, and technologies shelter clients from the effects of attrition. The providers in this research also discussed how their internal human resource policies, like offering interesting career paths, keep turnover low. A Senior Manager said his turnover rate in India is half the average turnover rate. He described why: *'The reason the team is successful and has a low turnover, presently, is the combination of good leadership (which is what the present leader brings), the benefits package, and the quality of work. We've got good pay packets and we've got good benefits. We're not overworking them to death. Some of these LPOs do do that.'*

## 3.9. **Relational governance**

*'We are treating them like a partner rather than thinking of them as a supplier.'* – General Counsel

Relational governance is the unwritten, informal mechanism designed to influence inter-organisational behavior. Relational governance is about the *attitude* clients and providers hold about the other and about the *behaviours* with which they treat each other. All of the clients in our LSO research talked about the importance of treating the provider as a partner. The partnership *attitude* manifests itself in partnership *behaviours* – such as resolving service issues together and conflicts fairly – that result in high performance from both client and provider perspectives.

### Practice 24: Treat the LSO provider as a partner, not a vendor

Prior research[11] found that strong relational governance begins with an *attitude* we call the 'Partnership View' in which a client regards the provider as a strategic partner rather than as an opportunistic vendor. LSO clients in this research specifically referred to their LSO providers as partners or teammates:

*'They are very flexible, they're very keen to learn, so they're not sticking to the letter of the contract. And so they do recognise it's a partnership'* – General Counsel

*'I think treating them truly as a partner on the team, a team member versus a vendor that we are trying to beat up on price every time we are talking to them.'* – Director

*To make this work, we wanted the Belfast team to feel like they were part of our team even though they are in a different country. We have done quite a*

*lot of bringing them into our family and making them feel at least like first cousins, if not like brothers and sisters.'* – General Counsel

The Head of Managed Services for a provider also described the close relationship he has with his client. He said, *'It's really a feeling of we are all on the same team, we're all living in the same environment. Our team leader goes to the client's legal team meetings. We participate just as if we are another unit within the legal department.'*

## Practice 25: Resolve issues and conflicts together

All service organisations have service issues, defined here as a circumstance which interrupts performance. Service issues, which include service lapses, project delays, or difficult people, are common and occur in any service, regardless of sourcing option. In our interviews, we asked participants to describe a significant issue and how it was resolved. Below we give one example of an issue caused primarily by the provider, two examples of issues caused primarily by the client, and one issue caused by both parties. In these LSO relationships, partners didn't focus on blaming the source of the issue but rather on working together to resolve issues. All the parties viewed the issues as a normal part of learning to work together.

One client asked the provider if it could support foreign languages. The provider indicated that they could support foreign languages from their Indian delivery centre. After a trial period, it became apparent that the provider had never supported foreign languages from this location before, and the result – according to the client – was 'quite disastrous'. The partners agreed that the provider would stop providing foreign language support. The issue has not weakened the LSO relationship, but rather has served as a valuable lesson.

On a large legal matter, one client severely under-estimated the number of lawyers the LSO provider would need to staff for document review. Although the client recognised that it was their fault for under-estimating the volume of work, they praised their LSO provider for working with them to address the problem. First, the provider more than doubled the size of the staff within four weeks of the engagement. But as the project neared its completion deadline, both parties realised they still did not have enough resources. The client and provider decided that working overtime was the best way to meet the deadline. The client and provider were sensitive about demoralising and burning out the LSO provider's staff, so they made the overtime work voluntary. The client also paid for the employees' transportation, security personnel, and facilities management costs for weekend shifts. 80 per cent of the LSO provider's employees volunteered and the project was completed on time. The client said, *'We have jointly identified that if something is not working that well, if it is clunky, we'll pretty much come up with a solution.'*

One client tried to assign new work to the provider without developing the playbook and processes first. The client wanted the provider to 'make their best attempt', but the client was not happy with the result. The provider reiterated that the nature of LSO work is different than assigning work to an external law firm and that LSO providers rely on processes, playbooks, and technologies to deliver quality service. The client learned his lesson and never by-passed the on-boarding process again.

On another account, the contract requires that the LSO provider will create playbooks by a certain date. Both the client and provider recognise that the volume of work has been so great, that the LSO provider is spending all their time doing the actual work, leaving little time to develop the playbooks. The GC said, *'They are peddling as fast as they can with the work that is coming in but they are now finding it quite challenging to do the playbooks and the commoditisation.'* The client and provider are discussing ways to resolve the issue, which will likely be that the client pays for an additional person focused on developing the playbooks.

## 3.10. Location of LSO staff

*'We need a provider here in the UK. We need a nearshore provider. We have a lot of volume business in Germany, France, Spain, Italy, and Benelux... There aren't many LPO providers that I've come across who are providing services out of those areas. I think there is an enormous opportunity.'* – General Counsel

When many people think of LSO, they assume all the work is done in low-cost areas like India, the Philippines, or China. Amongst our cases, the bulk of the LSO providers' employees are located in low-cost areas, but increasingly providers have also built delivery centres located closer to clients. LSO providers in our study recognise that large global clients need offshore, onshore, and nearshore alternatives. Global coverage can speed turnaround times by offering clients multiple shifts, balance the clients' cost and service requirement objectives, and offer multilingual support. Providers in our study recommended the following practice:

### Practice 26. Take advantage of a provider's global delivery capability

Each of the providers in our study discussed their location strategies and how these locations benefit clients. One provider locates about two-thirds of its LSO employees in India and about one-third in the United States. It also has small teams located in the UK and Asia Pacific. It operates its own data centres to run its proprietary tools and to store and protect client data, if the client chooses hosting services. The bulk of the work gets done in India but it is common to include onshore and offshore resources to service a particular client. For example, one client has a contract with the US Department of Defense that requires US citizens to perform any work associated with the contract. The provider said, *'It can be a mix of onshore and offshore so that the client gets the quality that they're looking for as well as a cost effective solution.'* For some clients, the provider runs double shifts – one in India and one in the US – without having to make employees work overtime or odd hours. For one client, a provider supports multiple languages including English, French, German, Italian, Spanish, Japanese, and Portuguese.

One provider uses a multi-shore model with two delivery centres located in India and three delivery centers in the United States. By using a multi-shore approach, the provider aims to deliver high quality services at the most reasonable price given the size, scope and deadlines of a matter. During the interview, the Senior Manager discussed in more detail the decision to locate a delivery centre in Minnesota to provide French language support. He said: '*We wanted French LPO support but France and Quebec don't look too hot when it comes to cost. We can't give French support out of India because French positions in India were handed back in 1954 and nobody speaks French anymore. So, that doesn't work. I actually suggested that we try and locate a provider in Romania or Poland, but we don't have enough work to sustain that. I said, "Okay, we can do it out of Minneapolis then."'* Minneapolis has four large law schools and its proximity to Canada means that many lawyers speak French. The challenge with any LSO delivery centre that provides French language support is that the French language differs across locations like France, Quebec, and non-Quebec Canada. He concluded by saying, regardless of location, *'We excel at the quality of work that we do. We are very good at what we do in the delivery of the work. It is one thing we don't compromise on: quality.'*

Another provider in our study has four major delivery centres, two of which are located in the United States, one in India and one in

Northern Ireland. The provider created a dedicated delivery team in Northern Ireland to service one client and both the provider and client are delighted with this location. The provider reports that *'Belfast has great access to talent including a bunch of folks that have moved from Belfast to London to pursue their legal careers and have had training with great firms and, for lifestyle reasons, are looking to move back home which is exciting because then when you get these folks, they tend to be geographically stable and loyal. We really like Belfast and the Invest Northern Ireland guys were great with working with us there.'* The client reports a 30 per cent cost saving by locating staff in Northern Ireland, partially because Northern Ireland offers great tax incentives.

A third provider in our study locates most of its employees in India, but it also built delivery centres in the United States to support foreign language work and work that clients want done onshore. The provider built one delivery centre in Utah because the Mormon population learns many foreign languages as part of its missionary work. In addition, the Mormon population is highly educated and has a tremendous work ethic. Although the costs are much higher in Utah than India, the set of capabilities adds great value for clients. For one complex legal matter, the client wanted to assign work to the provider's Utah and Indian facilities. The Director from the client company explained: *'With this particular case we were doing, it had some nuances so we thought it might be good to have some US attorneys. We wanted to test the Utah facilities. It was a good experience and opportunity for us to work with the US facility. So, I thought it was valuable.'*

## 3.11. Conclusion

The recommended practices discussed in this chapter pertain to LSO strategy, LSO provider selection, stakeholder-buy-in, contractual governance, transition and co-ordination of work, provider turnover, relational governance, and location of LSO staff. The lessons learned by the five companies in this chapter will be likely re-learned in many other enterprise legal functions as they too explore alternative approaches to sourcing legal services. It is important to note, however, that the LSO narratives at these companies are still being written and undoubtedly new lessons will continue to emerge from further experience. We aim to follow their stories as they continue to unfold.

1  Part I, Lacity, M., and Willcocks, L. (2012), *Legal Process Outsourcing: LPO Provider Landscape*, The Outsourcing Unit Working Research Paper Series, available at: http://www.outsourcingunit.org/WorkingPapers/WP12_5.pdf (accessed July 2013).

2  The specific examples we present in this chapter are from in-house counsels because those were the people who participated in our interviews, but the practices apply to both in-house counsels and external law firms.

3  We do not report provider revenues because three of the four providers do not disclose revenues.

4  Chandler, A. (1962), *Strategy and Structure: Chapters in the History of the American Industrial Enterprise*. Cambridge, MA: MIT Press.

5  See Susskind, R. (2012), *Provocations and Perspectives*, A Working Paper submitted to the UK CLE Research Consortium.

6   See for example Nagel, T., and Murphy, M. (1996), 'Structuring Technology Outsourcing Relationships: Customer Concerns Strategies and Processes,', *The International Journal of Law and Information* Technology, Vol. 4, (2), pp. 151–76.

7  These practices are from Lacity, M. and Willcocks, L. (2013), 'Beyond Cost Savings: Outsourcing Business Processes for Innovation', *Sloan Management Review*, Vol. 54, (3), pp. 63–9.

8  Lacity, M., and Rottman, J., (2012), 'Delivering Innovation in Outsourcing: Findings from the 2012 Outsourcing World Summit', *Globalization Today*, March, pp. 26, 31.

9  Lacity, M. and Rottman, J. (2008), *Offshore Outsourcing of IT Work*, Palgrave, United Kingdom.

10  See Carmel, E., and Tjia, P., (2005), *Offshoring Information Technology: Sourcing and Outsourcing to a Global Workforce*, Cambridge University Press, Cambridge; Krishna, S., Sahay, S., and Walsham, G. (2004), 'Managing Cross-Cultural Issues in Global Software Outsourcing', *Communications of the ACM*, Vol. 47, (4), pp. 62–6. Lacity, M. and Rottman, J. (2008), *Offshore Outsourcing of IT Work*, Palgrave, United Kingdom.

11  Lacity, M., Solomon, S., Yan, A., and Willcocks, L. (2011), 'Business Process Outsourcing Studies: A Critical Review and Research Directions,' *Journal of Information Technology*, Vol. 26, (4), pp. 221–58.

# Chapter 4

# Navigating the LSO Journey

## 4.1. Introduction

There are many fascinating aspects to how the legal sourcing model has evolved and will evolve in the future. The fact that it is a viable market at all is a major achievement. Just think: it is one of the riskiest elements of a business to outsource; it inherently involves the buy-in of one of the most risk-averse functions in a business; there are at least three players in the game (law firms, LSO providers, technology providers, etc.) rather than the usual two; it includes inherent barriers to outsourcing such as the need for qualifications for specific activities and jurisdictional constraints; and it involves people whose natural inclination is to deny that any of their work can be described as a 'process'.

Whilst these make legal processes one of the most challenging areas to outsource, it also means that when organisations get it right, then the benefits are significant. If LSO is to realise its full potential in the market then providers, law firms and clients must play their part in equal measure. The market is shifting between being provider-led and, as is currently the case, client-led. Only when all these elements are in balance will the market truly achieve its tipping point.

## 4.2. Evolution of the legal sourcing model

There has been a lot of noise made about the fact that the LSO market had, already, reached its 'tipping point'. This claim was backed up with plenty of well-publicised examples from law firms and General Counsels who were actively using LSO providers across a range of tasks. It is clear that there now exists a credible and workable solution to the requirement of wanting to outsource transactional legal work to low cost centres. But, does that mean the LSO tipping point has been reached? Actually, something has happened – the question has changed.

Or, to put it more accurately, the market is changing. The tipping point that everyone is actively chasing is actually moving further away as the dynamics of how organisations use LSO are changing. This is reflected in a wider trend within outsourcing generally where 'outsourcing' itself is no longer a stand-alone activity but is more-often-than-not part of a larger transformation programme or strategic imperative. So when General Counsels (GCs) are thinking about how they can respond to the increased workload, fewer resources and shorter timescales, they do not immediately think 'I need to outsource': they think about how they can transform their departments using a variety of different tools and approaches, one of which might be outsourcing.

This means the problem is approached from a different perspective, and the usual way that LSO vendors engage with their prospective clients ('What process would you like us to carry out for you?') is no longer valid. With the power more firmly on the client side (because they have taken the time to understand their strategy and map their processes) it is the GCs who are asking questions such as: 'I have all these processes, why should I outsource them to you?'

That change in perspective is driving different models, or 'eco-systems', that are being built around the in-house team. Some organisations are building their LSO relationships through their law firms and some are building Centres of Excellence around technology solutions, whilst others are building internal Shared Service Centres with integrated LSO capability.

The danger to be navigated by the LSO market is that it doesn't get stuck in a vortex of ad-hoc projects all chasing cost savings targets, and, instead, actually achieves 'escape velocity' to become a mature and viable sourcing solution for all large organisations that will deliver much more meaningful benefits such as scalability, increased responsiveness and risk reduction.

This chapter, as a whole, aims to give some sense as to how legal service outsourcing could evolve in organisations to become that critical business activity. The evolutionary journey will require some sort of map to guide it and give it some much-needed structure. That journey will also, inevitably, meet many challenges, some of which will be disproportionally amplified simply because of the unique dynamics of the legal market. These challenges, which are discussed in detail in Chapter 1, include heightened risk averseness, jurisdictional requirements, lack of process maturity, limitations of a consensus management, qualification requirements, provider market structure, predominantly an offshore model, tactical rather than end-to-end projects, focus on cost reduction, continual market development and maturity, relatively small provider base, lack of data and experience, and specialist technologies.

These challenges can, of course, be overcome. It requires a determined focus on the three key aspects of change management, sourcing and organisation. Any outsourcing will, of course, change the way that people do their work. Re-engineering processes is almost the easiest part of the whole thing – much more challenging is doing this whilst bringing everyone along with the reasons for the change. The change management aspects of any project or programme should aim to do this on an individual level, a team level and an organisation level, working to change the behaviours, mindsets and even culture of the function. As pointed out earlier, doing this within a legal department adds significant challenge to this activity.

The sourcing aspects, as well as running a credible and robust sourcing process, should always look to maximise leverage throughout the lifecycle. The world of LSO makes this more challenging because of the relatively small number of credible providers (compared to ITO and BPO – see Chapter 2) and, if required, the lack of true global capability. There is also a tendency to focus on short-term requirements (which is necessary to gain momentum and deliver quick benefits) but these need to be carefully balanced with the longer term aims of the function to ensure that any effort now is not wasted, and is aligned with those long-term objectives.

From an organisational point of view there are various stages of unrest that need to be gone through before order can be bestowed. The first of these is the unbundling of the legal processes that are carried out within the function. This unbundling activity is a process in itself and has to meet the challenges described above head on. However, once these processes have been identified and mapped, they can be applied to a 'standard' model or framework that will then help inform the sourcing strategy (what to outsource, how to outsource it and when to outsource it) and organisational design (ensuring that all of the different parties providing services to the function understand their roles and have the capability to carry them out as part of a legal 'eco-system').

The journey for any organisation implementing LSO will draw on all three of these aspects, in different degrees and at different stages. Understanding that journey is a key element to the success of LSO adoption in a company.

## 4.3. **Legal process framework**

In order to provide the necessary structure, the LSO journey will first require a map. That map is best presented in the form of a legal process framework to which the 'unbundled' processes can be applied. The framework takes a similar conceptual approach to many other process hierarchies but has the additional feature of a hard threshold between activities that require legal qualifications and those that do not. A basic framework is shown in Figure 4.1, below.

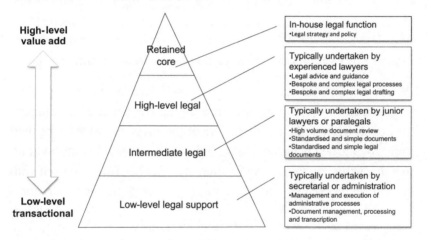

*Figure 4.1: Legal Process Framework*

One of these models would be applicable to each team within the Legal Function, each with its own specific activity groups. Every law firm or legal department will be different (they may, or may not, have a large Intellectual Property requirement, for example), therefore the make-up of these models will be specific to that particular organisation (see Figure 4.2).

*Figure 4.2: Legal Process Framework Across Departments*

Below each of the activity groups in each department are described the processes that are actually carried out. The process 'unbundling' can be described at a number of different levels, but each group will typically include between 1 and 25 processes associated with them. A whole legal department could therefore end up with between 100 and 300 processes identified.

Each of the processes can be assigned to a particular level within the hierarchy. So, for example, the process to renew a patent will sit in the Patents group of the Intellectual Property function and will likely be of an Intermediate level complexity, whereas the process to create a patent will have a High-level complexity.

Once the framework is understood, it can be 'sliced-and-diced' in a number of different ways, with each representing a different approach to how the work in the department can be outsourced. Each perspective will deliver a different sort of outcome and will carry with it different risks and benefits. For simplicity, the three most common approaches have been described here, with further detail given later. In the example diagrams below, each triangle represents one function (such as IP, Corporate, Property, etc.) within a legal department, and the shaded areas those that have been outsourced.

Managed Legal Service is the most sweeping of the different approaches described, where a whole team and all its work are outsourced. It includes the transfer of all levels of activities, apart from the core strategic decisions (Managed Legal Services outsourcing is depicted in grey in Figure 4.3).

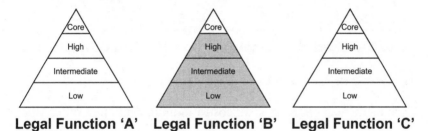

**Legal Function 'A'    Legal Function 'B'    Legal Function 'C'**

*Figure 4.3: Managed Legal Services*

With a Vertical Slice approach, all Low, Intermediate and (potentially) High aspects of one 'low impact' area of legal work are outsourced (see Figure 4.4). 'Low impact' refers to an area of activity that carries a relatively small amount of risk and would therefore not materially impact the business should it fail.

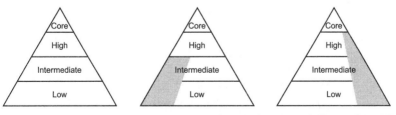

**Legal Function 'A'    Legal Function 'B'    Legal Function 'C'**

*Figure 4.4: Vertical Slice of Legal Activity*

A Horizontal Slice approach looks across the different legal functions to unbundle and outsource a specific process which is relatively transactional and can be standardised across the teams (see Figure 4.5).

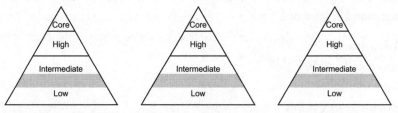

**Legal Function 'A'    Legal Function 'B'    Legal Function 'C'**

*Figure 4.5: Horizontal Slice of Legal Activity*

Each of these approaches is described in more detail below.

## The managed legal service model

A more nuanced picture of the managed legal service model is depicted in Figure 4.6.

**Approach:** The outsource provider would take over all aspects and activities of the function, excluding the overall strategy and ultimate legal responsibility.

**Example:** The entire Employment team can be outsourced as a managed legal service. On a smaller scale, this could also be just the Immigration team, for example.

**Provider interfaces:** The provider would implement best practice processes and technologies within the function, interfacing with the clients own processes and technologies only where appropriate.

**Locations:** Some processes within the function may be carried out offshore and, where confidentiality isn't an issue, between shared teams.

**Pricing:** Pricing could be on a fixed price, or per key volume basis (e.g. number of employees).

**Advantages:** it minimises interfaces between client and provider; it is easier and quicker to make changes to the process; the provider can implement best practice processes across the whole function; the provider can exploit their own technologies to manage the function; pricing mechanisms are simple.

**Disadvantages:** A perceived loss of control of a legal function or team; a feeling of 'detachment' from the core business; a resulting dependency on one provider; the inclusion of outsourcing of potentially higher-risk activities; it can take a while to set up.

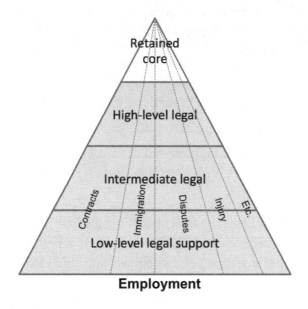

*Figure 4.6: Managed Service Legal Model in Detail*

## Vertical slice of legal activity

See Figure 4.7 for a more detailed example of the vertical slice of legal activity model.

**Approach:** The outsource provider would take over all of the low risk/low impact aspects of the activity within the team, excluding the overall strategy, ultimate legal responsibility, high risk/impact activities, and, where appropriate, legal opinion.

**Example:** The low risk/low impact Discovery (eDiscovery and Manual Review) activities in the Litigation team (but not the high risk/high impact litigation Discovery work).

**Provider interfaces:** The provider's processes and technologies would interface with the client's own, particularly where matters move from Intermediate to High levels.

**Locations:** Some processes within the function may be carried out offshore and, where confidentiality isn't an issue, between shared teams at the provider.

**Pricing:** Pricing could be on a per key volume basis (e.g. number of documents) or as Full Time Equivalents FTEs required.

**Advantages:** Relatively low risk approach; suitable for project-based work or activities with high variability of volumes; relatively easy to set up and implement; a good starting point for LSO adoption; only pay for what is used.

**Disadvantages:** Some interfaces (and therefore risk) as matters move between Intermediate and High levels; there is a need to determine the risk level of activities prior to outsourcing, and this may change over time.

*Figure 4.7: Vertical Slice of Legal activity Model in Detail*

## Horizontal slice of legal activity

Figure 4.8 depicts a horizontal slice of a legal activity model in more detail.

**Approach:** The outsource provider would unbundle the elements of the processes that include the outsourced process.

**Example:** Contract Attribution and Filing activities across all relevant teams.

**Provider interfaces:** The provider would implement a best practice process (with technology where appropriate), interfacing closely and seamlessly with the clients own processes.

**Locations:** Some or all of the outsourced process may be carried out offshore and, where confidentiality isn't an issue, between shared teams.

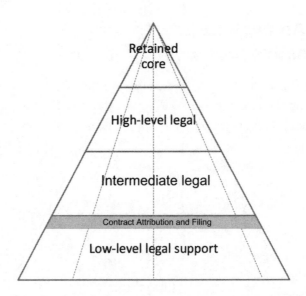

*Figure 4.8: Horizontal Slice of Legal Activity Model in Detail*

**Pricing:** Pricing could be on a per key volume basis (e.g. number of contracts) or by FTEs required.

**Advantages:** It achieves common and best-practice processes across the whole department; it removes laborious processes from the workload of highly qualified people; client you only pays for what is used.

**Disadvantages:** It is relatively complex to set up and implement; it is suitable for very transactional, high volume processes.

Each of the above approaches has, as described, a distinct set of benefits and risks. Of course, these are not mutually exclusive approaches to take, and they can be combined into more complex strategies. Of particular interest to this chapter is how these approaches can be used as part of an evolutionary journey to implement, and then increase, the adoption of LSO within an organisation, such that the maximum benefits are realised at the lowest risk.

## 4.4. **An evolutionary approach: alternative journeys**

Although any of the three sourcing models can be implemented straight off, there can be a lower risk evolution of the services to an ideal model. This evolutionary journey can take a number of different paths, and with different end points, and each of them will depend on a number of factors, such as the organisation's appetite for risk, the existing structure of the department and the nature of its business. Three such journeys are described in Figure 4.9.

The logical place to start is with the lowest risk approach – this allows a period of development and learning that will not unnecessarily impact the business if there are any failures in the process. The outsourcing of a 'low impact' process in one legal function, such as a non-critical eDiscovery project or the ongoing renewals of non-critical patents allows the organisation to become familiar with the arrangements but, importantly, provides a suitable foundation to increase adoption throughout the department (if that, of course, is what the sourcing strategy has been determined to achieve).

The first approach to increasing adoption (marked as 1 in Figure 4.9) is for the provider, once they have proved themselves capable, to take on responsibility for higher value (not necessarily higher risk) tasks within the existing scope of work. In the eDiscovery example, this could mean the provider taking on greater responsibility for the manual document review at the end of the process, or, in the patent renewal example, it could mean the provider being involved in the decision process of whether certain (low impact) patents need to be renewed. All of this, though, would still be within the 'low impact' work which formed the initial scope.

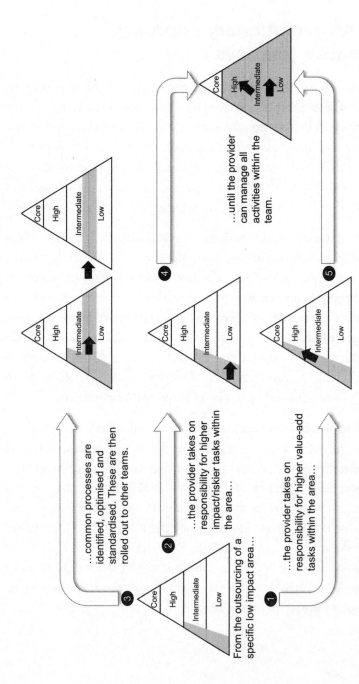

*Figure 4.9: Potential Evolutionary Outsourcing Journeys*

One alternative to that approach is to increase the scope of work by including 'higher risk' activities but within the same process (marked as 2 in Figure 4.9). For eDiscovery this would mean the provider doing the same work as before but on matters that would potentially have a higher impact on the business. For patent renewals, it would similarly mean the provider processing higher-impact patents.

A third approach is to pick one or more 'common' processes out of the existing scope (marked as 3 in Figure 4.9) and extend the outsourcing of these to other functions. In the two examples used so far, this could simply be some elements of document management. Other examples could be contract attribution (the extraction of key attribute meta-data from all contracts) across the full scope of contracts used in the department. This particular journey can be carried out in stages (do one function, then another) but, to realise the full benefits of a standard, best-practice process, it is best to determine what the final scope might be.

Once these initial increases in LSO scope have been taken, there are further steps that can ultimately lead to the outsourcing of complete function within the legal department (or even the whole legal department itself). These are marked as 4 and 5 in Figure 4.9 and describe the combining of approaches 1 and 2, i.e. moving to higher value and higher risk activities in the existing scope, and then repeating that for other areas within the department.

This then raises the important question of how to know which is the most appropriate journey for any particular organisation. There are a number of important considerations that will inform this decision.

The first of these is the need to understand the objectives of the department. Every department will have different objectives to different degrees, whether it be building scalability, improving responsiveness, increasing flexibility, reducing costs, or some combination of these. In order to determine what these are it is beneficial to understand first what the main drivers of change are – generally these can be categorised into internal and external, and proactive and reactive factors. For example, as shown in Figure 4.10, an organisation may have ambitious growth plans that will put severe strain on the legal department (Internal, Reactive) but at the same time it may want to be seen as an employer-of-choice (Internal, Proactive). Similarly, its competitors may be becoming more aggressive with respect to their stance on IP (External, Reactive) but the business wants to get its products or services to market quicker (External, Proactive).

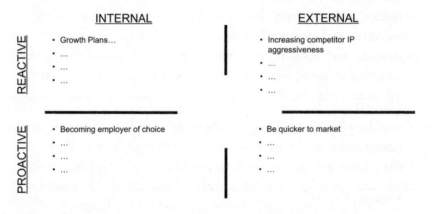

*Figure 4.10: Drivers for Change*

Understanding these organisational drivers for change will help determine the objectives for the department, and therefore the appropriate path to adopt with respect to legal outsourcing.

The other key consideration is the outsourcing journey in the context of any wider transformational activities. Although legal process outsourcing has, to date, been carried out as a distinct activity, it should ideally be implemented as part of a transformation programme. The departmental objectives that have been developed are more likely to be fully addressed when people, processes, organisation and technology are considered holistically, with outsourcing as one important element of this.

Typically, a transformation roadmap can be developed which aligns the outsourcing changes with the process and system changes, as shown in the example in Figure 4.11.

All of the above activities, across systems, processes, organisation and people, can be organised into four streams of work in order to manage the transformation programme:

**Manage**: To put in place, where they don't exist already, the fundamental departmental capabilities to manage and control the workflow and costs, and measure its performance. This could include elements such as Performance Management, Spend Management and Vendor Management.

**Standardise**: To standardise all relevant processes and tools to improve efficiency and enable shared working. This could include the introduction of templates and best-practice common processes across the department and into the business.

**Source**: To source the most appropriate providers at the best value, ensuring that they all work seamlessly toward a common goal. This could include LSO providers, law firms, technology vendors and paralegals.

**Optimise**: To put in place the enhanced departmental capabilities and processes to fully optimise control, efficiency and flexibility of the department. This could include Knowledge Management, Matter Management, Performance Management and Demand Management.

Developing a full transformation roadmap, based on the departmental objectives, considering all of the dependencies between people,

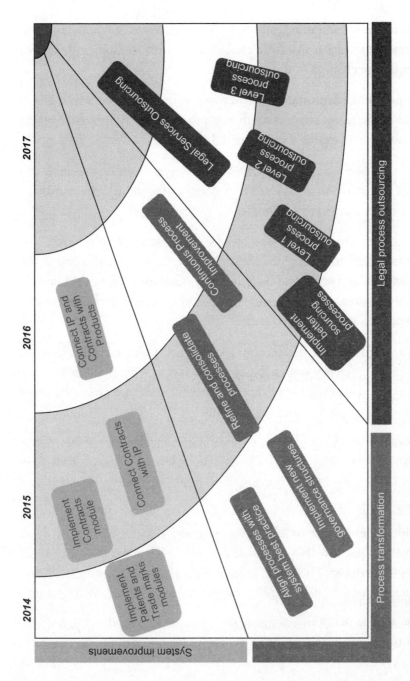

*Figure 4.11: Example Legal Transformation Roadmap*

processes, organisation and technology, and organised into these four streams, will inherently drive out the relevant evolutionary journey for the specific LSO approaches described earlier.

The evolutionary approach to LSO, based around a robust framework and strategy, focuses primarily on providing direct benefits to the business in terms of delivering labour arbitrage savings at low risk, but it also enables organisational change that can enhance the capabilities of the department itself.

## 4.5. **The legal ecosystem**

The most important of these benefits is the ability it brings to develop a legal 'ecosystem' around the core in-house counsel resources. This could involve a number of third-parties or internal teams, all providing a seamless 'platform' of services to the in-house counsel. By identifying, collating and allocating, through the use of the legal framework, all of the activities that are best carried out by third parties or internal shared service teams (either because they are very transactional, technologically enabled or highly specialised), it allows both the department to scale as business activity increases, and for the core in-house counsel team to focus on the high value, business critical activities. Figure 4.12 summarises this approach.

In order to maximise the 'business partnering' benefits, the service platform needs to be designed and implemented so that it optimises and streamlines the processes and technologies as much as possible. Again, this can be put into an evolutionary context to ensure appropriate risk mitigation and future-proofing.

Different sourcing strategies can therefore be developed around how the service platform ecosystem is constructed and ultimately evolves. Three innovative approaches are described here.

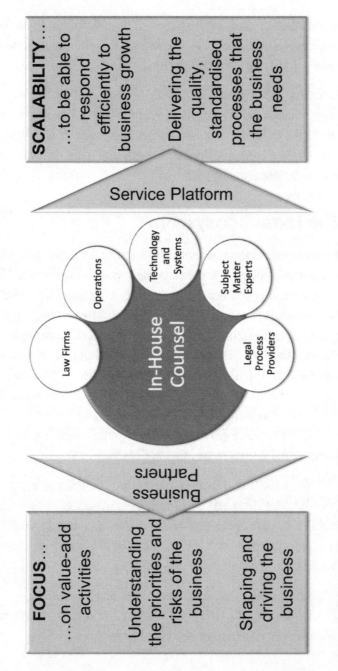

*Figure 4.12: Legal Ecosystem*

The 'Hub Model' involves the introduction of a number of LSO providers focusing on specific types of matters or geographies (or both). Having more than one LSO provider provides some healthy ongoing competitive tension between each of them, as well as mitigating some of the risk if one of them happens to fail in some way.

For 'full service' legal departments or law firms, it is often best to have at least two providers managing different aspects of the legal work (IP and Contracts, for example), because they can exploit specific expertise in each area. For global organisations, it may be a good idea to have one provider for each major region covered (e.g. US, Europe, Asia) which then negates the need to select only providers with global coverage. Each of these types of 'hubs' can act as gateways for the relevant matters and provide a good balance of onshore and offshore capability. Indeed, starting the LSO journey close to home can mitigate many of the initial risks and fears, and a gradual migration of the appropriate work to an offshore (low cost) delivery location can then realise more of the labour arbitrage benefits.

Figure 4.13 shows the concept of a geographically aligned hub model, whilst Figure 4.14 shows this aligned to types of matters.

The triage function, which assesses the incoming matters so that they are directed to the most appropriate resources, can be provided by the provider, as shown in these examples, or by the client, which creates additional models and opportunities for competition.

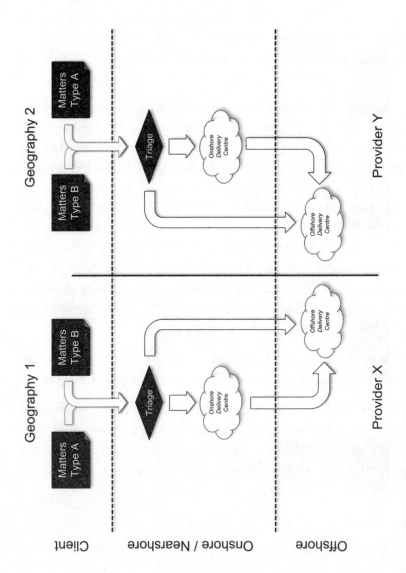

*Figure 4.13: Geographic Hub Model*

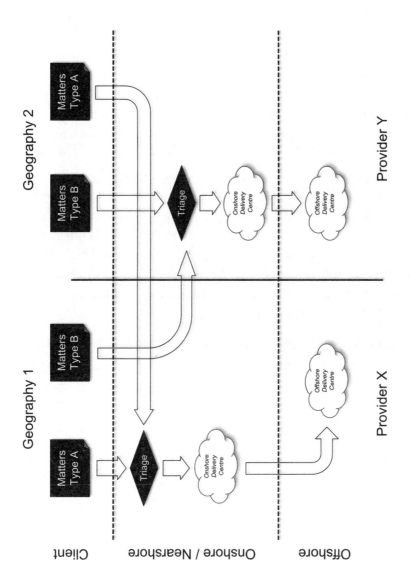

*Figure 4.14: Functional Hub Model*

## 4.6. Conclusion

As discussed at the start of this chapter, most of the existing LSO work is carried out on a project-by-project basis, or, if it is done long term, it tends to be for very specific processes. The opportunity to contract on a 'services' basis rather than a 'process' basis, though, provides significant opportunities to maximise the benefits of using third parties. Legal Services Outsourcing differs from LPO in that it tends to involve significant consolidation from ad-hoc relationships with multiple law firms into a strategic relationship with one or a few, and will cover all legal work for a particular organisation or practice area. The strategic law firm provider will receive guaranteed work volumes in return for significantly lower rates. The main contracting party tends to be the law firm, but there needs to be tight integration with the other third parties including LSO providers and technology providers. In this way much of the risk is passed to the law firm. These are the same principles as outsourcing of other centralised functions such as IT and Finance.

A precursor to this sort of arrangement is the unbundling of the processes and the application of the organisational framework, including the departmental capabilities such as Performance Management and Demand Management.

The ultimate evolution of the framework is the creation of an Alternative Business Structure (ABS) where a large organisation may 'spin out' an internal legal transactional capability, in order to provide that service direct to its customers. The need to carve out specific processes and functions for the ABS means that the framework needs to have been addressed previously and evolved to the point where the processes are fully documented and optimised.

In all areas of business, but particularly in the legal sector, the rate of change is increasing dramatically. Whilst the provider market is maturing and developing in many different directions, the clients' buying experience is expanding and expectations are increasing. Meanwhile regulatory changes create both barriers and opportunities to progress.

It therefore makes sense to approach LSO as a journey, evolving and aligning the organisational model as these other aspects develop and mature. To create and evolve the necessary ecosystem takes both vision and detailed planning. It means thinking strategically about transformation whilst unbundling individual processes. It means planning a long journey on a constantly changing map whilst ensuring that everyone is okay every step of the way. It means thinking big whilst acting small. The legal department and law firms will survive only if they are the fittest they can be, and the evolution of the LSO market is an inherent part of that journey.

# Chapter 5

# In Their Own Words

## 5.1. Introduction

Whilst researching this book, we had the privilege of speaking with and formally interviewing many thought leaders on the topic of legal transformation and the role of LPO/LSO there within. In previous chapters, we analysed, synthesised, and aggregated the lessons from many research participants, but in this chapter, we invited nine thought leaders to be heard *in their own words*. We are pleased that leaders from enterprise legal functions, providers, and an external law firm contributed to this chapter (see Table 5.1). These individuals are essentially the creation of the LSO landscape. They are constantly adapting its features as lessons are learned and most importantly, as capabilities are built.

For thought leaders representing enterprise legal functions or law firms, we asked them to answer the following questions:

- What is the current status of LPO adoption in your organisation?

- In what ways does/might LPO add value to your organisation and to your clients?

- What do you foresee as the major challenges and opportunities for LPO in the next three to five years?

- What advice would you give other law firms or in-house counsels considering LPO adoption?

*Table 5.1: Thought leaders contributing in their own words*

| Voice of the: | Name | Title | Company |
| --- | --- | --- | --- |
| Enterprise Legal Functions | Christian Sommer | Group Legal Director | Vodafone |
| | Gawie Nienaber | Former Associate GC, CSC | Independent |
| | Richard Tapp | Company Secretary and Director of Legal Services | Carillion |
| Legal Services Providers | Mark Harris | CEO | Axiom |
| | Liam Brown | Founder and Chairman | Elevate Services |
| | David Holme | Managing Director | Exigent |
| | Bob Gogel | CEO | Integreon |
| | Dan Reed | CEO | UnitedLex |
| Law Firm | Alex Hamilton | Principal | radiant.law |

We repeat that the terms LPO and even LSO do not label accurately all the providers in this chapter, as companies like Axiom are best seen as an alternative 'new model firm' and many providers offer consulting services and other high-valued work. Thus, we first asked thought leaders from the provider firms to describe their services. Then we asked about their views on LPO. The specific questions were:

- Besides cost savings, what value do your LPO services add to your clients?

- Are there any misconceptions about legal process outsourcing that you would like to clear up?

- What do you foresee as the major challenges and opportunities for LPO in the next three to five years?

The responses are below. At the end of the chapter, we summarise the insights and identify common threads. We start with the views of thought leaders in enterprise legal functions.

## 5.2. **Christian Sommer, Group Legal Director, Vodafone**

 Christian Sommer was born in 1967 in Essen, Germany. Christian studied law at Albert-Ludwigs-University in Freiburg, Germany and at Université de populaire de Lausanne, Switzerland. He specialised in international contract law and corporate law. Christian started his in-house legal career in 1996 at the group legal department of Mannesmann AG supporting the international engineering division of the company. In 1999 he helped to set up the legal department in the newly formed telecommunications division of Mannesmann (Mannesmann Eurokom GmbH). In 2001 Christian joined the Vodafone Group legal department where he held several roles supporting the M&A and franchising activities of the Vodafone Group. Christian is admitted to the bar in England and Wales, Germany and the Czech Republic and holds a qualified bank clerk certificate. Christian is currently responsible for the legal support of Vodafone's procurement, technology and R&D activities.

*What is the current status of LPO adoption in your organisation?*
In Vodafone I would see us currently at the half-way mark in terms of LPO adoption. We started a couple of years ago with the implementation of a vertical LPO solution (end-to-end responsibility for the LPO provider) supporting a dedicated part of a centralised business segment. This year we have enhanced this approach by

adding a horizontal LPO support model (work-type defined responsibility for the LPO provider), again for a centralised business unit in our group. What is still missing (and clearly forms part of our future agenda) is to look into ways of adopting/extending any of the existing solutions so that they could be used to support decentralised areas of the business as well as for the legal support of demands generated in any of our 20+ local markets. The difficulty we are faced with here is that different legal regimes apply and different laws would have to be supported by any LPO provider. What we are therefore currently looking into is the creation of pan-European contracting principles and standards within our Vodafone legal community. Once this step is completed, we will run a feasibility study with a number of LPO providers to see *what* can be done via LPO and *how* it needs to be done so that it can support our heterogenous customer base.

### In what ways does / might LPO add value to your organisation?

LPO does certainly add value to Vodafone on a number of levels. Firstly, it can indeed be taken as a tool to control/lower the cost base of an in-house legal team. Contrary to what people might think now, I do not necessarily refer to the basic 'get the same work done cheaper outside' principle. LPO the way we use it in Vodafone generates cost efficiencies by segmenting the type of work we cannot/don't want to do in-house anymore and find cheaper alternatives via LPO so that, bottom line, our legal department costs decrease. Secondly, LPO as described above enhances the capability level of our in-house legal teams. By taking away certain (low complexity) work the in-house lawyers concentrate on high value and high complexity work which reduces (a) the need to hire external law firms (cost saving) and (b) enables us to constantly improve the skill-set level of our legal employees and by doing so, to keep know-how within the company and to create a diverse and interesting job environment for our people.

Lastly, I also see LPO as a tool to strengthen the standing of an in-house legal department within any company. External law firms and internal specialist teams (litigators, competition lawyers etc.) usually have a strong reputation because they are working on specific and often complex legal tasks. Commercial lawyers sometimes are taken as 'a given' dealing with any kind of non-specific query. The segmentation of work as part of a LPO does help to raise the awareness amongst the client base of what, how and when in-house legal support is needed and impacts positively on the standing of the commercial lawyer as well.

### What do you foresee as the major challenges and opportunities for LPO in the next three to five years?

I expect the LPO market to grow significantly over the next three to five years. For the reasons stated above I assume that a lot of GCs will (have to) look into alternative ways of running their legal teams whereas LPO is one of the potential changes some of them will be likely to adopt. I also expect the variety of offerings from LPO providers to grow and to become more diverse over that period. This will be partly in response to the different demand patterns based on the legal system the LPO needs to support but also because of more complex (and maybe also more expensive) work packages LPO providers would like to address with their offering. This could also become one of the challenges for LPO going forward. In case LPO develops into more complex areas the likelihood for any LPO-based legal support to be challenged in court (or via arbitration) will increase significantly. This could potentially be the starting point for damages claims being brought to LPO providers by their customers which would have an impact on the overall business case (and the offering landscape) for any kind of LPO. I do believe that we currently don't know where risk and compliance milestones are when using LPO. But I am convinced that we will know at the end of that three to five year period.

*What advice would you give other GCs considering LPO adoption?*
My advice would be to identify the reason(s) for considering LPO clearly before starting such a significant project. Often LPO is looked into for reasons a LPO adoption will not help to change. Once the real drivers (cost reduction, segmentation of work, behavioural change programme) are identified, my second piece of advice would be to start with a pilot project covering a limited area of the legal support spectrum first before 'going big'. Doing so helps a lot to fine-tune the working relationship with the LPO provider before the LPO becomes system critical and also to convince internal stakeholders that the LPO solution is the right thing to do. My final but most significant piece of advice would be: Don't underestimate the amount of internal support any kind of LPO will require from you and/or your team. To make LPO work you will have to invest a lot of time and effort (not just for the pre-kick-off period but also during the ongoing LPO operation). GCs sometimes tend to believe that the LPO provider will take care of any difficulty when performing LPO services but this does not take into account that the GC and her/his team are the link between internal customers and the LPO provider. Therefore, they are the most relevant element for making LPO a success.

## 5.3. Gawie Nienaber, Former Associate GC, CSC

Gawie Nienaber joined CSC in 1993 as Senior Counsel and after various expansions in his role was appointed as Vice President and Associate General Counsel. CSC is a NYSE-listed hardware-independent global provider of technology services including applications, IT infrastructure, Cloud, Cyber, Big Data, and proprietary software solutions, with revenues of $16 billion. He left CSC at the end of 2012. His primary role was to support the business and operational needs of CSC's business in EMEA. Until 2008 he managed CSC's EMEA legal team and from 2008 he also managed the legal staff in CSC's International Legal Group which supports all CSC's non-US geographies. He has law degrees from the University of Stellenbosch, University of Oxford (which he attended as a Rhodes Scholar) and Harvard Law School. He is admitted as an English Solicitor and an Attorney in New York and Washington DC.

### What is the current status of LPO adoption in your organisation?

At the outset the term 'Legal Process Outsourcing' requires unpacking. In its narrower, conventional meaning the 'Legal Process' being outsourced refers to certain document intensive or quasi-mechanical tasks (for example, in litigation discovery, patent applications, M&A document review and legal research) that historically would have been performed within law firms by more junior or para-legal staff. The advent of Indian and other lower-cost locations has allowed these tasks to be performed at a lower hourly rate, albeit not necessarily at the lowest overall cost.

In my experience and based on input from Tech Sector GCs, for IT companies these transactional-based services have had an unequal take-up. For those providers with a rich patent portfolio the take-up has been higher; for others, more limited.

For some IT service providers the 'Legal Process' that has been outsourced has a broader meaning and indeed is no longer a 'legal' process. IT service providers who enter into long-term managed service agreements with clients to take over aspects of their business processes such as information technology have a requirement to identify, manage and monitor obligations embedded in the services agreement. For CSC the most developed LPO implementation to date has related to contract obligations management, initially a fully outsourced service performed by an Indian provider and shifting over the course of the last 2-3 years to an Indian-based in-house organisation managed within the CSC Contracts function.

IT service providers have also to different degrees embarked on outsourcing supply chain support, that is, moved the support for the procurement function previously performed by the in-house legal function to an external or in-house Indian-based provider or function. Others have sought to outsource the production of standard contracts (such as business to consumer contracts).

The pace with which senior in-house lawyers are being encouraged by the business leadership to look across the whole range of legal services to consider what can be done in lower-cost locations is undoubtedly increasing, but implementation varies.

### In what ways does / might LPO add value to your organisation?
If properly structured, managed and invested-in LPO can add substantial value to an organisation in cost and efficiency terms.

In the broader sense of the term LPO sits in a continuum of services stemming from the fragmentation of the traditional legal services model. Under this approach, due to technological advances facilitating the entry of lower-cost providers and economic forces dictating the need for lower cost service provision, the conventional law firm with its pyramid operating structure is no longer at the centre of legal service provision but rather is increasingly being marginalised by alternative legal service delivery models such as Axiom and the so-called virtual law firms.

In the narrow sense of LPO (repeatable task-based activities entailing the application of templates or rigid guidelines and requiring minimal supervision, client interaction or exercise of legal or business judgement) the market is becoming clearly established and it will be a question for an organisation to determine if it has the scale and nature of business to take advantage of the portfolio of offerings by LPO providers. I would posit that in this sense of LPO the take-up cannot be ubiquitous across all organisations.

In the broader sense of LPO (looking to best-of-breed legal service providers to cover the full range of legal demands placed on an in-house legal team, with selection based on optimised cost and capability criteria, and suppliers mainly located on-shore) my view is that LPO can benefit all organisations, large and small.

*What do you foresee as the major challenges and opportunities for LPO in the next three to five years?*
Macro-economic factors will come into play. India may lose its ascendance in cost terms but may balance that with increasing capability. This balancing act will apply across other jurisdictions.

Regulatory or technical barriers such as dealing with attorney-client privilege arising from transferring privileged information to LPO providers will likely be overcome.

More profoundly, the effect of the economic downturn has not only increased the demand for more cost-effective legal services but also unleashed a supply of high quality lawyers both in private practice and in-house who have either become disaffected with the conventional law firm model or been released by law firms or corporations under cost pressure. This pool of talent is available to the new market entrants who can provide an equal service on-shore at substantially lower cost. In that sense I anticipate higher growth for on-shore LPO than offshore LPO over the next year or so. Offshore LPO is also traditionally constrained by its inability to deploy its offerings in civil law jurisdictions. On-shore LPO is not.

A significant challenge for GCs will be to have a cohesive vision and LPO strategy. Optimal implementation of LPO does require a considered assessment by the in-house legal team of the services it currently provides, a good understanding of the capabilities in the market that can satisfy demand on a lower cost/higher value basis, and clarity of the demand that can be outsourced. It may also require clear choices to be made between choosing lower cost options where the risk of failure is mitigated, and the converse will apply as well. And once assessments have been made the challenge will be to choose a strategy and then execute against it. None of this is easy. However, even then, the major challenge to implement LPO holistically will be institutional inertia.

***What advice would you give other GCs considering LPO adoption?***
In the narrower sense of LPO (where the service is provided offshore) careful consideration should be given to whether your organisation has the scale and type of service that can systemically take advantage of LPO.

Care should be taken with offshore LPO services that are a hybrid between applying templates or rigid guidance and requiring judgement, such as contract drafting support for the Procurement function. In practice these are difficult to specify, supervise and implement cost-effectively.

In the broader sense of LPO (deploying low-cost best of breed services both onshore and offshore across the full range of legal capabilities that an in-house team need to have or procure) there will be inevitable pressure on GCs to consider blended in-house and externally provided services. So apply your mind and prepare a business case. It is better to do it yourself than have others do it for you.

## 5.4. Richard Tapp, Director of Legal Services, Carillion

Richard leads the legal team at Carillion plc, a FTSE international integrated support services business with annual revenues around £5 billion. He also has responsibility for a number of other corporate teams, and for Carillion Advice Services which provides a range of new managed legal services offerings and resources, including the largest provider of telephone advice services under the legal aid scheme.

He has led a range of innovative legal sourcing arrangements for Carillion, including the formation and development of the Carillion Legal Network. He is the co-author of Managing External Legal Resources (ICSA). Before joining Carillion plc in 2001, for six years he was Company Secretary and Group Legal Adviser for Blue Circle Industries PLC, a FTSE 100 global heavy building materials business. He has established, run and integrated in-house legal teams in North and South America, Europe, Australasia, the Middle East and Asia.

*What is the current status of LPO adoption in your organisation?*
We started to adopt LPO some five years ago, cascading process work from our in-house legal team and data room and contract work from our legal network law firms to one of the major global outsourcers in India, and litigation document work to the US office of the outsourcer.

Since 2011, we have developed our own in-sourced LPO/managed legal service provision, with a paralegal centre of more than 60 people based in northern England – Carillion Advice Services (CAS). CAS has allowed us to map and unbundle significant amounts of work from our in-house legal team, and from our legal network law firms.

We are currently putting a range of work into CAS, from employment and contract review, through to data room work and litigation management, and it is a condition of the law firm's membership of our legal network that they put work which is capable of being done by the CAS team into the centre.

A number of network law firms are also now using CAS to service their own non-Carillion client base, and we have a joint offering with one of the firms in employment law, which we believe to be unique.

### In what ways does / might LPO add value to your organisation?

Directly, our use of CAS allows us to reduce legal costs – using our paralegals to replace law firm paralegal, trainee or junior legal resource brings significant financial savings – but also allows us to systemise elements of the work bringing efficiencies and economies of scale, together with quality benefits.

It also allows us to introduce its services into Carillion's broader outsourcing offerings to our clients, to use it to work with our suppliers to allow them to improve and reduce the cost of their offerings to Carillion, and to offer the service to third party clients, allowing us to demonstrate one of Carillion's core values of innovation.

CAS is also one of the largest providers of telephone-based legal advice to the UK legal-aid scheme, and provides benefit advice to the customers of major utility companies as well as our own consumer clientele. In so doing, it builds on our sustainability goals by developing advice offerings to a broad range of individual clients through initiatives such as web-based advice, advice to our clients with hearing difficulties through sign-language, and a language line for non-English speaking clients.

*What do you foresee as the major challenges and opportunities for LPO in the next three to five years?*
We see major challenges in the provision of legal advice generally – the regulatory and economic environments continue to be challenging, whilst at the same time the cost of advice to businesses becomes unaffordable, and public funding of advice to individuals continues to reduce.

These drivers require major change in the way legal advice is sourced, and LPO and managed legal services represent tools for the legal profession, LPO providers and clients. They will require openness of thought and delivery on the part of all three to develop new and collaborative ways of working which identify and recognise whether a problem requires legal input at all, whether it can be solved through existing resource, and if it does need legal input which elements can most effectively be provided by the client themselves, the provider, or the profession.

We see one of the key challenges – and opportunities – as the development of solutions which address these drivers whilst allowing the ultimate client to receive seamless delivery. A disjointed offering, lacking clarity of accountability or bringing with it issues around language, time zones or cultural understanding reduces the take-up of an offering and threatens the achievement of the benefits.

The challenges and opportunities are both cultural and technical – they require new and different ways of working, and also the means of sharing knowledge, work process and work product seamlessly across teams.

***What advice would you give other GCs considering LPO adoption?***
There are two key issues to remember:

- GCs are best placed to develop the optimal solution for their organisation; and

- LPO is a tool, a resource available to the GC in delivering that solution.

To expand further, GCs know the structure and culture of their business, the legal risks which it presents, and the strategy which it seeks to follow. No two organisations are the same, and GCs can use this critical know-how about their business to design the model they use for providing legal advice to suit the legal risks, business drivers, organisational design and culture of the organisation.

Within that, LPO is a resource, as part of the options available to the GC. The mix of legal provision to consider in the make-or-buy decision has become a lot more complex in recent years – not just the question of do you do work in-house or put it to a law firm, but can you provide it through expert systems, can you standardise or systemize it, or can you avoid it altogether?

The GC will want to ask all those questions, and only then consider the mix of in-house, law firm and LPO work. It is vital to map out the key elements of our legal work – if necessary with the help of appropriate consultancy skills – to determine which pieces are best done by which provider. The driver for LPO may be to control costs, but it is also essential to maintain the quality, effectiveness and timeliness of advice. The GC will also understand that the organisation will hold them accountable for delivery, however they choose to source the advice.

As such, a GC needs an LPO provider which can demonstrate its innovation, its ability to work with in-house teams and law firms to provide a single solution. It must have quality systems which work, and which can be accessible and flexible in their delivery route. In short, it must be willing to work with the GC to devise the right solution for the organisation.

## 5.5. **Mark Harris, CEO, Axiom**

Mark Harris is the Founder and CEO of Axiom, a 1000-person new-model legal services firm that serves nearly half of the Fortune 100 across eleven offices and four delivery centres globally. Purpose-built for the efficient execution of sophisticated legal work, Axiom is the world's largest and fastest growing non-traditional provider of legal services and is the recognised leader in legal industry innovation, having been ranked number one in innovation 'in the business of law', 'in corporate strategy' and 'in law firm efficiency' by the *Financial Times*. Prior to founding Axiom, Mark practiced law at Davis Polk and Wardwell and clerked on the US Court of Appeals for the Ninth Circuit. He received both his BA and JD from the University of Texas where he served as President of the Texas Cowboys Honorary Service Organisation.

Before answering the questions, Mark wrote us the following preamble: Important note: *Axiom does not self-describe as an LPO. Instead, we consider ourselves a new model firm. Please see answer three for greater context.*

***Please briefly describe the major legal services your organisation provides.***
Axiom is a new model legal services firm that enables Fortune 1000 clients to 'insource' seasoned lawyers or 'outsource' complex legal functions from our ten offices and four delivery centres around the

world. As such, we are the world's largest and fastest growing non-traditional provider of legal services. We are the only sophisticated, end-to-end provider of corporate legal services that is not a traditional law firm. The ability to handle the entire value chain of work – from routine to complex – uniquely differentiates Axiom from traditional LPOs.

### Besides cost savings, what value do your LPO services add to your clients?

Axiom does, in fact, save clients a significant amount of money. We have stripped out 50 per cent of the cost-structure from the delivery of sophisticated legal services, which enable rates that look too good to be true but aren't.

Interestingly, however, the primary motivation for our clients is not usually cost (though that is always a bi-product of innovation). It is, instead, better risk management and repurposing high-value senior team members.

Better risk management comes from clarifying desired outcomes – through clear policies and guidelines – and putting the necessary processes, tools, and quality control procedures in place to ensure adherence to those policies and guidelines. And it comes from delivering better insight into the positions that have been taken, so that the company is better able to respond to changes in the marketplace (such as new regulation or a changing financial landscape) when they arise.

Freeing up members of the in-house team to focus on more strategic and higher value matters enables proactive risk control and policy creation, which is the non-delegable responsibility of the internal law department. It often also enables the law department to take work back in-house that was being sent to external law firms simply because the in-house team lacked the capacity to do the work (rather than because the law department needed the unique skills or imprimatur of the law firm). The business benefits from a better investment of time as in-house lawyers are stacked against more strategic work. Since that work is more valued by the end-client and since it is more interesting, the law department benefits from higher team satisfaction, which eases management challenges.

### *Are there any misconceptions about legal process outsourcing that you would like to clear up?*

Perhaps the most common misperception is that Axiom is an LPO. We are not, at least in the traditional sense. Let me explain: LPO, in common vernacular in the industry, is work that lends itself to being executed by junior people in offshore low-cost geographies. The offshore model is employed by all the 'LPOs' – it is their origins. Therefore, this is work that a) is only about process b) requires little/ no business or legal judgement; (c) prohibits any legal advice or practice of law due to local/foreign regulations and d) includes no direct interaction with corporations' counterparties.

While we recognise that we compete against traditional LPOs for some work, we do not define ourselves as one because of:

- Sophisticated legal work, end-to-end: The work we do covers a spectrum of sophistication: at the high-end, we are displacing the use of law firms in a given area; at the mid-high/medium point on the spectrum, we are doing work that used to be done by senior company lawyers; and we will also handle the lower-end work if it is a part of the same value chain. The bigger picture here is that we control and deliver on the 'end-to-end' value chain.

- Client motivation: Our client's primary motivation for using Axiom is not cost (as with an LPO), but rather risk management or the desire to redirect senior in-house talent.

- Lack of capability limitations: The sophistication of what we take on is limited only by a client's willingness to outsource, rather than by our capabilities.

### *What do you foresee as the major challenges and opportunities for LPO in the next three to five years?*

We think that the traditional LPO model faces significant challenges and opportunities over the next five years. While we hate to answer a question with a question(s), that approach may be warranted here:

- Is the traditional LPO model valuable? Yes.

- Is it going to transform the industry? No.

- Why? If you map the value chains in different practices (as we have done), the work that lends itself to this approach is less than 10-15 per cent of the hours. As many GCs have said, LPO work is breadcrumbs.

- If LPO work is breadcrumb work, then what gets to the meat? The model that we think is more transformative is the wholesale, end-to-end outsourcing of entire *legal* functions – again, the entire value chain approach.

While traditional LPOs are intent on moving upstream, into the type of complex work Axiom regularly tackles, they will need to:

- Establish a near shore (US/ Europe) presence/talent pool

- Establish a talent brand in the West among top legal talent

- Establish a reputation for legal/business judgement quality (vs. processing)

- Establish trusted relationships with big company GCs/ DGCs

## 5.6. Liam Brown, Founder and Chairman, Elevate Services

Liam Brown founded Elevate (www. elevateservices.com) in 2011 to provide corporate legal departments and law firms with practical consulting, managed services and technology solutions to improve efficiency, quality and outcomes. Previously he was the Founder, President and CEO of Integreon, Inc. (www.integreon.com), which he led from start-up in 2001 to annual sales of nearly $150 million by 2011. Under his leadership, Integreon pioneered the global delivery of high-value legal, research and business services and technology to 32 of the Am Law 50, all of the top 10 global investment banks, 9 of the top 10 life sciences companies, 6 of the top 10 technology companies, and 17 of the top 50 global brands. Liam has twenty years of experience in the legal services industry, primarily serving law firms, investment banks and Global 1000 corporations. Prior to Integreon, he was the President, Chief Operating Officer (COO) and co-founder of Conscium, a web-based virtual deal room serving lawyers and bankers, which he sold in 2001 to then-NYSE-listed Bowne & Co. Liam is also an active investor in Web 2.0 and Cloud technologies, and an executive coach for founders of startups (www.forwardinnovations.com).

*Please briefly describe the major legal services your organisation provides.*

Elevate offers corporate legal departments and law firms practical ways to improve efficiency, quality and outcomes. We provide consulting, managed services and technology solutions.

Our consulting teams help corporate legal departments improve the technology and processes of their operations and analyse and benchmark their spend with outside counsel to improve the value they receive.

We offer a range of legal support services to corporate legal departments and law firms, which allow them to do 'more for less', such as document review, contract management, due diligence, intellectual property, and medical claims and litigation services. We also offer law firms a range of business support services, which allow them to reduce their overheads, such as procurement services, word processing, IT, HR, marketing and business development and finance and accounting services.

And finally we offer legal project management software to law firms to help them scope, set and manage to achieve their matter budgets.

*Besides cost savings, what value do your LPO services add to your clients?*

Our services not only reduce cost, but also improve outcomes for our clients. Take our medical claims and litigation service, which expedites settlement and reduces damages for our clients. Recently a plaintiff claimed that he was hit in a parking lot by one of our client's trucks (a Fortune 100 company). He had four surgeries, past medical bills of $578,000, and demanded $2.15 million. Our legal and medical staff used our patent-pending systems to analyse and audit the plaintiff's medical history and records, recommended that the medical bills for 'usual and customary' treatment for injury related to the accident should have been $115,000, helped the defense counsel assess the case early on, as a result of which the defense offered a $400,000 settlement. The settlement offer was refused so our expert witness testified at trial and the verdict returned was an award of only $270,000. Our invoice to our client was less that $10,000 – which was less than 10 hours of law firm partner time, and an almost $2 million reduction in damages!

### *Are there any misconceptions about legal process outsourcing that you would like to clear up?*

Language is powerful and I wish we would change language, despite the convenience of the term 'legal process outsourcing'. First, let's stop using the term 'outsourcing'. When a corporate legal department sends legal work to a law firm it is not called 'outsourcing' to a 'vendor'. Second let's stop using the term 'process', which implies that the work travels along a conveyor belt. The reality today is that some legal work is practice of law and some is not. Practice of law is the domain of the profession, but legal work that is in support of the practice of law, i.e. 'legal support', can sometimes be unbundled, automated or otherwise systematized, still requires judgement, and can be provided by what I call 'alternative legal services providers'. Is Axiom Legal a law firm, an LPO or an alternative legal services provider?

The ethical arguments against legal support are a smokescreen. Lawyers cannot brush aside or try to find a way to work around the ethical obligations associated with legal support. If the ethical obligation of the lawyer is to put the client's interest first, is it really in the client's best interest to have a law firm resource a document review on Friday evening by asking which five associates are free because they need to review a due diligence file by Monday, rather than staffing with the three associates that have the expertise and experience to do the work most efficiently? It's an extreme example that we all know sometimes happens, but it's no more extreme than the stories you hear about alternative legal services providers in India staffing a document review with people who have never done legal work before, which we have all heard about. My point being, I think it is wrong for alternative legal service providers and law firms to make extreme arguments about the other. What I found successful time and time again was to have the law firms very involved in the sampling and oversight of the alternative legal service provider work in a systematic manner – simply fulfilling their ethical obligations.

Recently it has become fashionable for some law firms to build an 'LPO Captive' and claim 'it all needs to be performed under one roof', citing the difficulty of unbundling, project management, the quality benefits of control, clashes with culture, etc. In my experience this is usually nothing other than lipstick on the pig of the old pyramid structure. I support law firms actually making the investments in technology and process expertise required to 'work differently' and improve the efficiency of legal services, but it is not good enough to continue to bill for junior lawyers by the hour whenever a GC lets them, by claiming to 'do the work in-house in our LPO Captive', and even worse to use that as a smokescreen for winning business and then largely delivering the service the way the firm always has. Instead, I'd like to see the law firms invest in project management and unbundling – getting at the heart of having the right people, with the right skills, doing the work in the right place. When pressed on the economics, the business outcomes, and the quality of the work, some law firms claim these can't be measured. However, there are many examples of measuring and managing knowledge work that have been implemented in many professions and as soon as you start to do that for legal work then you start to see opportunities for improvement. I can name numerous law firms that have fundamentally reduced their costs; that are paid higher rates per hour by their clients; that involve their lawyers in oversight of alternative legal service providers; and that achieve higher-quality, repeatable, defensible outcomes. Think about that for a minute: the client's overall fees go down, but the law firm actually generates more profit than before; their lawyers no longer spend their time on rote work, and they have a systematic way of overseeing quality and consistency of the work. Everyone wins.

***What do you foresee as the major challenges and opportunities for LPO in the next three to five years?***
There are a couple of notable challenges. The first is that a lot of venture and private equity capital went into the industry in 2006 and now those investors are looking to monetise their returns. That causes alternative legal services providers to operate differently to how they did in the first five years of the industry's existence. They're now less inclined to invest in the long-term because their investors are focusing on near-term returns and liquidity. This creates a challenge to their clients and employees – client service has suffered and clients have started to vote with their feet. I believe it is a mistake to focus on near-term returns and liquidity in serving the legal market, where relationships between a company, its law firms and its alternative legal services providers are not just a series of mutually exclusive transactions; but rather more an ecosystem where all parties are looking for mutual gain over the long term.

The second challenge relates to the alternative legal services providers remaining stuck in the paradigm of 'we need to look like our clients so they trust us, but do the work at lower cost'. They've been hiring lawyers in low cost offshore locations, but doing the work in a similar way to how their clients' lawyers have done so in the past – or how their clients have told them to do it. This has resulted in the stigma of offshore labour arbitrage rather than process re-engineering and systematization of the work. I think the evolution of alternative legal services will be to true consulting, technology, and process re-engineering, i.e. disaggregation of steps in the legal system and its frictionless reintegration. It's going to deliver defensible, repeatable, sustainable, measurable and improvable outcomes.

I don't think 'LPO' will be a term ten years in the future. It's an acronym that we use today to distinguish between the delivery of advisory legal services and the delivery of non-advisory legal support services. In the future I think we will see lawyers much more focused on a professional advisory role – really adding value, which is aligned with what the corporate legal departments truly care about. 'LPO' will simply represent the non-advisory legal support work that will be variously performed sometimes by the corporate legal department, sometimes by the law firm, and sometimes by third party alternative legal services providers.

## 5.7. David Holme, Managing Director, Exigent

David is an ACA who had a 14 year career in the City of London with global institutions including KPMG and Bridgepoint. At Bridgepoint, a $5 billion fund, David led the investment group responsible for investing in support services. David went on to establish Exigent in 2003. Exigent is now a leading provider of consulting, LSO and LPO to leading global law firms and corporates. Exigent now employs 300+ staff globally and has six offices in five countries. David is a Chairman and founder of Exigent responsible for driving the strategy of the business.

*Please briefly describe the major legal services your organisation provides.*

Exigent provides Shared Services, Legal Services and Consultancy Services to law firms and large multi-national corporates.

'Shared Services' are services traditionally referred to as 'back office' support functions, of which Exigent offers the following: document production, creative design, bid support, marketing administration, compliance support, knowledge management, finance and HR administration.

Legal Services typically requires qualified resources, and includes document review, due diligence review, contract services (management, review and drafting), global supply chain contract management, legal research and assistance, case assessment and claims handling, policy reviews, IP portfolio management, lease review and management, and knowledge management services. The scope of these services is growing very quickly with three new service areas added in as many months.

Consultancy services are designed to improve delivery through increased process efficiency or lower delivery cost, or both, and are provided by Exigent's process consultants.

*Besides cost savings, what value do your LPO services add to your clients?*

In the early '00s' LPO depended upon wage arbitrage but Exigent has always considered this to be a weak and short-sighted strategy, especially as systems and processes improve. We continue to look to innovate in each of these various ways: People (legally trained and numerate), training (business process and legal training), process (all staff are required to understand lean delivery), IT (detailed knowledge of all platforms), and sector specialisation are all complementary to delivery. Adopting these techniques allows Exigent to price with certainty.

We attempt to identify areas where clients are resource constrained as well as where cost pressure is an issue; many clients need help seeing where these areas are. We then build the appropriate model for delivery using the key principles set out above. An example might be multi-lingual contract management where large multi-nationals can centralise this function and deliver consistent quality to several jurisdictions or the management of global supply chain contracts for a mining corporation.

A further example might be the systemization of delivery of various services through the development of consistent delivery with targeted SLAs. This allows for predictable turnaround times and consistent quality across regions, thereby reducing risk.

Quality people will become more important as the business migrates up the value chain. Many LPOs design rigid processes to support lower-skilled staff. We believe this to be an outmoded delivery method in the more advanced areas. Quality people supported by process and measured by productivity is a quite different model to process being the foundation with quality people being the value add. For corporates and law firms alike this adds a vital component in more complex areas where the brief may change and not necessarily fit a rigid process.

### *Are there any misconceptions about legal process outsourcing that you would like to clear up?*

We believe context is important. Legal fees rose by 20 per cent more than the average rate of inflation for services in the UK in the years prior to 2009 (see PwC legal services report 2012). Law firms simply left a gap in the market and clients acted rationally by looking at alternative delivery models.

Many commentators believe that LPOs are the same. LPO has become an acronym (before it's time), which carries with it a range of preconceptions (cheap labour, limited offerings, commodity work only): Some are related to outsourcing, some to legal, most are way out of date.

The industry is evolving far faster than the law firms and is more in tune with the corporate agenda which means that in the future there will be greater choice. By contrast law firms are retrenching and variously trying to innovate at a much slower pace than LPOs. Sadly, most law firms believe that 'innovation' is an award, not a deliverable.

All law firms have a series of tasks, not 'processes'. Exigent mapped 120 processes in a major law firm in 2013. So process must exist especially in a fixed fee environment. This widens the scope for remote process-based delivery.

A significant misconception is that LPO 'do process' and law firms deliver bespoke advisory; this is a mistake. Our recent work demonstrates that there are multiple processes or sequential tasks. This allows LPOs to target up to 30–40 per cent of the tasks that a law firm undertakes. This means new firms such as RocketLawyer or radiant.law can simply outsource considerably elements of work without building offices and overhead.

*What do you foresee as the major challenges and opportunities for LPO in the next three to five years?*
The challenges will be significant and illustrative of a market that is likely to change more in 20 years than the last few decades. There are few precedents.

**Challenges:** There are too many small scale LPOs, especially in India; many will fail. A larger firm may fail and the recent contract losses in the UK undermine the industry; competition, new entrants/ ABS legislation. We view this as creative disruption. This is positive. Law firm reaction e.g. paralegal centres onshore.

Poor law firm management of outsourcing – OC/CMS/Integreon may well be an example of joint failure, not a failure of outsourcing. In a conservative market this can be a 'told you so' moment; this misses the point. Other flexible delivery models leveraging contract lawyers.

**Opportunities:** Continued and increased pressure on law firm margins will force law firms to change and clients to demand more pricing flexibility and efficient delivery in most areas of law; the cat is out of the bag. In 2012, 50 per cent of law firms restructured banking arrangements. Firms must change their operating model much faster. The lack of capital funding for investment in the partnership model will force firms to look at alternatives. LPOs will become trusted partners especially for corporates. Initial cynicism has faded and they are seen as legitimate players. Being part of an established and accepted landscape will open up new opportunities. Joint delivery with innovative law firms such as McCarthy Tetrault which is truly groundbreaking in Canada and will evolve rapidly now. This allows jurisdictional expertise and an exceptional brand, to be supported by process efficiency and scale at a fraction of the cost. Opening of internal corporate markets where a large proportion of spend is concentrated will continue apace. Low penetration rates for LPO providers with corporates will change; we expect a fourfold increase in this work in 2013. New geographies and sector specialisation is proceeding at increased pace. LPOs will adapt and deliver higher-level work, and leverage technology more effectively than traditional models. Their ability to act quickly and re-invest in delivery capability will drive exceptional growth.

## 5.8. Bob Gogel, CEO, Integreon

Robert (Bob) Gogel has over three decades of experience as both a provider and purchaser of global outsourcing, technology and consulting services. Before joining Integreon as CEO in July 2011, he held a number of CEO roles and executive board positions at world-class organisations and has been active in developing onshore, near-shore, and offshore service delivery centres, including extensive experience in building teams across multiple countries and cultures. He has also worked closely with and for private equity firms, multinational companies, and the public sector. Bob is co-founder of a leading think tank – the European Executive Council (EEC) – the editor-in-chief of The State of the European Union annual conference, and a member of the faculty teaching the MBA programme at HEC in Paris and Shanghai. He holds a BA from Harvard, a Masters degree in Applied Economics from the University of Louvain and an MBA from the University of Chicago.

*Please briefly describe the major legal services your organisation provides.*
Integreon is widely recognised as a trusted provider of LPO to law firms and corporations around the world.

In general, legal outsourcing at Integreon is an operating model built upon a best practices framework, with process efficiency, quality control and enabling technology at its core. Our approach leverages years of experience, a global footprint, shared services, best of breed technologies and varied delivery models to provide first-in-class legal outsourcing support and transformational consulting services to law firms and corporate legal departments.

Integreon's discovery services include litigation and regulatory document review and end-to-end eDiscovery support including consulting, collection, processing, hosting and production. On the transactional side Integreon supports corporate clients with contract drafting and negotiation, contract data abstraction and the management of ongoing contractual rights and obligations. Integreon has also pioneered collaboration with outside counsel for the provision of end-to-end contract lifecycle management support. Other services include M&A due diligence, compliance, legal research, document drafting and immigration support.

We also offer deep consulting expertise for the design or re-engineering of legal processes. We work with clients to transform key elements of their operating models and have experience in building a broad range of sophisticated engagement and operating structures. These include onshore and offshore dedicated delivery centres, captive operations, and Build Operate Transfers. We also have a proven track record in successfully transferring staff from clients into Integreon and vice versa. This experience gives clients considerable flexibility with regard to location, ownership, and scale of operations. Our consultants will analyse legal processes and then provide advice around the optimal location and delivery model, the right mix and utilisation of technology, best practices, and the flexible resources required to address the challenges our clients face.

### Besides cost savings, what value do your LPO services add to your clients?

We enable our clients to focus on what they do best. Our services allow a variety of legal functions to be standardised, unbundled and broken down to their constituent elements so that resources can be allocated based on the complexity of each task. Routine work can then be automated or delivered by teams of professionals who specialise in these activities, enabling our clients' in-house lawyers to work more efficiently, with greater satisfaction, and focus on higher value tasks that are core to their role or business.

Our support can be delivered around the clock too. Integreon's global delivery platform spans four continents affording our clients 24/7 'follow the sun' delivery, including access to foreign language resources. Our Manila location, for example, offers lawyers fluent in multiple European languages and Asian languages including primary Chinese dialects, Japanese and Korean. Foreign language support is also available from our onshore US and UK locations.

While there is often a cost benefit, it is important to note our ability to help clients improve quality and save time. We do this by streamlining processes, developing metrics, specifying formal service levels, and applying smart technologies. We have a dedicated Quality and Continuous Improvement team of certified Lean and Six Sigma professionals who help to ensure our clients see improved performance year on year.

I'm proud to say that Integreon's LPO services are closely integrated into many of our law firm clients' own value propositions. The law firm's brand is enhanced. They are viewed as being cognisant of the cost, efficiency and quality demands of their own clients, and they gain a competitive advantage as a result. The law firm's expertise, together with Integreon's know-how in global LPO, process-based development and transition provide an overall service that is greater than the sum of its parts.

*Are there any misconceptions about legal process outsourcing that you would like to clear up?*
Even today, I still hear the accusation being levelled that inherent in the utilisation of LPO services is a greater degree of risk and that also quality somehow suffers. I refute this wholeheartedly. Our LPO services are provided under a model that by its very nature minimises

risk and assures quality (through extensive documentation, governance, performance metrics, KPIs and SLAs). Our Quality and Continuous Improvement team works hard to improve our processes so that we can perform faster and with fewer errors. We apply a rigorous regimen of quality control procedures across all of our LPO service lines. In the rare event that we should fail to meet an SLA, service credits can apply.

Some within private practice tend to view LPO as a threat. Our view is the polar opposite. We believe that innovative law firms that embrace LPO as an opportunity to differentiate their firm will actually enhance their own brand and gain market share as a direct result. Our strategy is to collaborate with law firms in order to help them provide better value to their clients. Our services free our law firm clients to focus more on higher margin work. I believe as the legal market continues to evolve, ABSs emerge, and value-based billing begins to dominate, the legal services delivery model of law firms must also evolve. At Integreon, we do not practice law and as such do not aim to cut out law firms from corporate law departments. Only by working together can we provide clients with an end-to-end, holistic solution in the 'new normal'.

Another misconception is that the only benefit LPO brings to the table is labour arbitrage. While this may have been true in the past, today what we term at Integreon as LPO 2.0 is characterised by deep collaboration between the key constituent stakeholders, namely law firms, corporate legal departments and LPO providers. Legal functions are now analysed and re-engineered based on whether they can be eliminated, automated, or allocated to lower cost resources.

*What do you foresee as the major challenges and opportunities for LPO in the next three to five years?*

The pace of technological innovation is an area that presents both a challenge and opportunity for LPO. New developments in technology-assisted review, automated contract meta-data abstraction, and document assembly technologies are speeding up or significantly reducing the necessity for manual labour. While LPOs routinely integrate technology, it is incumbent upon us to stay abreast of new developments and ensure we always bring the most innovative solutions to the table, even if this means throwing fewer bodies at a problem. At Integreon we've invested heavily in both proprietary and best of breed third party technology to support our eDiscovery, contracts and other LPO services. We employ technology-assisted review to create advanced workflows combining the best of both human and machine.

In addition, while unrelenting cost pressure, deregulation, disaggregation, globalisation and technological advances have been the genesis of LPO, over the next three to five years the challenge and the opportunity will be to develop new service delivery models that drive ever greater innovation. We believe that you can either shape the change taking place or be shaped by it. It is incumbent upon law firms, corporate legal departments, and LPO providers to find better ways of working together. In the coming years I have no doubt we will see even closer collaboration, with the lines of ownership of the legal services delivery model becoming increasingly blurred as these stakeholders invest in and enter into joint ventures with one another. Under this more integrated model our clients will see better management of the flow of global contracts and IP, improved compliance with burgeoning regulation, more effective control over litigation risk and cost, and the closing of M&A deals more quickly.

## 5.9. **Dan Reed, CEO, UnitedLex**

Dan's focus throughout his career has been on helping companies optimise the legal, financial and operational aspects of their businesses. Prior to founding UnitedLex, Dan served as Chief Financial Officer and General Counsel to Adjoined Consulting, and then as Managing Director of Kanbay International. Adjoined provided management consulting, integration and outsourcing IT services to a primarily Fortune 500 client base (Adjoined was acquired by Kanbay International, India's sixth largest IT services provider, for $225 million in early 2006). At Adjoined, Dan helped establish the company's unique brand of financial and legal execution while managing various offshore (India, Singapore and Malaysia) service provider relationships. Prior to his career with Adjoined Consulting, Dan was Vice President of Corporate Development and Legal Affairs at SmartDisk Corporation where he guided the company through early stage structuring and execution of its initial public offering, and was responsible for all offshore (Japan, Taiwan and the Philippines) shared services, corporate development activity and research and development activity from a legal perspective. Dan began his career 17 years ago with Ernst & Young LLP providing audit and tax advice services to New York City area companies. He then went on to Greenberg Traurig LLP (an AmLaw top 10 firm with more than 1,500 lawyers) where he represented venture-backed and Fortune 500 companies in the technology, financial, healthcare and manufacturing sectors.

*Please briefly describe the major legal services your organisation provides.*

UnitedLex is a global company with a single mission: to improve the performance of law departments and law firms. We provide unparalleled solutions to address the risk, efficiency and effectiveness goals of our clients in North America, Europe and Asia. Our company of more than 750 attorneys, engineers and consultants drive economies of scale and knowledge in the areas of litigation, contracting, intellectual property, general legal and operations to deliver seven and eight figure benefit to our clients. Founded in 2006 and with more than $250 million in assets, UnitedLex deploys the right blend of service and technology in supporting the world's leading corporations and law firms. UnitedLex is the only full service LPO recognised by Chambers and Partners as a Tier I/Band I legal service provider. A list of our major service offering has been provided below:

- Litigation Support

- eDiscovery Solution

- Early Case Assessment and Collections

- Data Management and Document Review

- Law Firm Solutions

- Intellectual Property

- Contract Management

- Financial Advisory Service

- Loan Trade Closing

- Commitment Management

- Obligation Management

- Legal Research

- Immigration

- Governance Services

- Global Language Support

*Besides cost savings, what value do your LPO services add to your clients?*

The LPO industry has moved beyond cost arbitrage and also scaled up the value chain. We have emerged as a high complexity services provider catering to a wide range of solutions like eDiscovery analytics, litigation readiness assessments, collections, expert witness services, patent drafting, patent analytics services, contract negotiations, and obligation management.

We are continuously trying to help our clients by delivering better and technically advanced business solutions. We have a huge competitive advantage of having our own Propriety Technology designed to fill gaps and serve niche requirements not addressed by third party systems (a combination of automated and human analysis of patent portfolio, obligation management, improved reporting and transparency during collections). Our ability to bundle technology with services offers a highly attractive proposition to clients.

*Are there any misconceptions about legal process outsourcing that you would like to clear up?*

As stated earlier, this industry is not just about cost savings and has been successfully able to add value to its clients' business by continuously evaluating their changing legal/business requirements and tailoring its offerings accordingly. Having said that, there has been a considerable shift in the way LPOs have been perceived. As we have been experiencing significant growth in this sector, we are now being seen as a specialised and knowledge-driven industry that combines deep domain expertise with a blend of technology and people processes to deliver success benchmarks in the legal arena. The industry is no more viewed as performing only simple and routine legal services. Our clients don't perceive us as a legal services vendor but engage with us on a long-term basis with strategic transformation objectives.

We are helping our clients reduce risk, improve consistency and efficiency through process standardisation and process improvement. Partnering with us also gives them a better control on certain specific service areas that we are equipped to deal with in a more specialised manner.

### *What do you foresee as the major challenges and opportunities for LPO in the next three to five years?*

There is a need for deployment of captive legal knowledge centres. The ability to recruit and retain the right talent is an enormous challenge for Global Fortune 500 companies. Getting the unique technology right is equally a challenge. UnitedLex is well positioned to address these issues and provide dedicated teams that foster efficiency and scalability – and enable companies to retain the vast amount of intellectual capital that is generated in these units.

Some of the trends that are evident are related to LPOs exploring non-traditional services like loan processing, litigation financing etc., and unlike earlier this competitive sourcing is now managed by procurement departments (RFPs, due diligence audits) from the client side. This in itself is a testimony that the business trend is evolving for LPOs. The demand for end-to-end integrated solutions (combining services, technologies, jurisdictional coverage) are increasing as the smaller players are being acquired (CrownBridge and LawScribe acquisition by UnitedLex) by bigger players to make the industry more competitive. Another visible trend is the interest that the

European, Australian, South African and Asian clients have been demonstrating in this sector.

The limitations can be classified as some of the challenges we foresee for the industry.

- LPOs will have to keep pace with the rapidly evolving technology and integrate it effectively into their services.

- The ability to leverage talent globally and effectively integrate global delivery capability will be essential to providing required solutions to clients.

- In addition, it is essential to effectively integrate technology, domain knowledge and process expertise to break the linearity of revenue and headcount.

## 5.10. Alex Hamilton, Principal, radiant.law

Alex Hamilton is a lawyer specialising in outsourcing and IT contracts. Alex co-founded radiant.law in 2011 as a new type of law firm, offering experienced lawyers, fixed fees and innovative service delivery. Before that, Alex was a partner at Latham and Watkins and co-chair of its global Technology Transactions Group. Alex has led five projects that have been recognised by the FT's Innovative Lawyer Awards and was shortlisted for the FT's 2010 Innovative Lawyer of the Year award.

*What is the current status of LPO adoption in your organisation?*
radiant.law is a UK law firm that was created to offer more cost effective and better value legal support than the large law firms that the founders came from. All of radiant.law's transactional support is offered on a fixed price or equivalent basis, which means that we are motivated and able to use the most effective way of supporting clients, rather than the way that maximises billable hours. We also specialise in outsourcing transactions, so are comfortable with the concept of outsourcing. We therefore have used LPO from our formation (the beginning of 2011) to provide the support that would normally be given by junior lawyers to the onshore partner-level lawyers.

We mainly use LPO to support us with more repeatable activities that require consistency, rigour and some level of judgement. The judgement requirement is key: we try to automate the truly rote tasks. Examples might be – 'review this document against a set of rules' or 'compare these documents and tell us the substantive differences'.

Clients know that we use an LPO provider, but all contact with the firm is with the onshore lawyers and we check everything and take full responsibility for the work carried out offshore. From our perspective, we see the LPO personnel as extensions of our team, who we are actively involved in training.

*In what ways does / might LPO add value to your organisation and to your clients?*
LPO gives us a number of competitive advantages, which traditional law firms will struggle to adopt (due to the way that they are motivated through billing time):

• We can scale our support as needed over time, without having to commit to taking on full time employees. At the same time, all our training is provided to the broader team at the supplier, so that we can invest in building the capability we will need in the future.

- As LPO is far cheaper than the cost associated with having onshore dedicated employees, LPO helps us offer highly competitive pricing to clients.

- We have also found that we can improve the quality of more routine activities, which LPO providers tend to be far more sophisticated (through process improvement) at performing than would normally be the case within law firms, where 'ad hoc' is the rule.

### What do you foresee as the major challenges and opportunities for LPO in the next three to five years?

One of LPO's biggest challenges is that it is not offering the (highly conservative) in-house market a 'whole product'. LPO can seem to be just too hard to adopt (other than for large discovery and due diligence exercises), given that it will require the heavy involvement of the in-house legal team. The multi-paragraph, all caps disclaimer at the bottom of every LPO stating that they aren't providing legal services does not help on this front!

We believe that there will be new market entrants (like radiant.law) offering clients legal service outsourcing where full support for an area of repeatable work is outsourced to a provider that is a regulated law firm. These providers will leverage LPO providers but offer the additional legal review, technology and client interaction that gives the client a full service. We see this as one of the great growth opportunities of the next five years.

*What advice would you give other law firms or in-house counsels considering LPO adoption?*

We are highly sceptical that traditional law firms will have the inclination or ability to take advantage of LPO. Despite what they might say publically, law firms will have to radically change their business and compensation models before they can use LPO effectively (other than where the client has twisted their arm on a particular project). We do not see this happening in a widespread manner in the next three years.

In-house counsel, however, is highly motivated to reduce work and save costs. The challenge is that there is a high investment and commitment needed to make it work. We would suggest starting by using LPO support of discovery or due diligence exercises, as these are straightforward and little different to taking on law firms.

## 5.11. Conclusion

The common themes across the enterprise legal function thought leaders were that they are still on the LSO journey. While the LSO pace is increasing, LSO implementation varies and in-house retained capability needs careful thinking through. They identify real LSO value in terms of cost efficiencies, support, and as an additional tool, while again stressing the role of the enterprise for clarifying and controlling its sourcing strategy. It is suggested that the regulatory and macro-economic challenges, together with the large pool of legal talent available, are accelerating the development of LSO services. The challenges, especially for offshore providers, will be dealing with complex legal tasks and providing seamless service. The advice is identify a clear business case for LSO, pilot using external services, choose LSO when the scale and type of service merits it, and build internal capability to deal with the changed sourcing and operating models.

Understandably, the provider thought leaders had a less cautious, more 'can-do' approach to the services they offer and towards future developments. They stressed the multiple services now available in the market, and that the LSO market now went beyond cost savings to include process standardisation and improvement, lowering business risk, releasing in-house expertise for higher value work, providing expert resources where needed, and facilitating a more flexible operating model. They saw a number of misconceptions, in particular highlighting that often they were a source of innovation and new technology for the industry, and a catalyst for change in the face of pressures on cost, service and operating models.

Alex Hamilton, the thought leader at the firm radiant.law, gave fresh insight as an LSO user citing the advantages of cheapness, scaling, and process quality improvements. He also saw his kind of law firm making LSO easier to adopt than when a client has to deal directly with the service provider. Given the growing pressures on clients with regard to cost, service and responsiveness, he saw a battle between these factors and client conservatism resulting in more LSO and use of firms like his own over the next three years.

The thought leaders expressed some differing opinions. For example, one thought that traditional LSOs could only ever replace 10 per cent to 15 per cent of a law firm's hours, while another thought that LSOs could target between 30 per cent and 40 per cent. Some saw low-level, repeatable processes as the only suitable work for LSO while others saw the service offerings evolving into much higher-valued and complex work. Across their varied voices, a number of harmonious opinions were expressed. First, although LSO is often seen as a threat to the profitability of law firms, thought leaders argued that through deep collaboration, all parties can gain from the service offerings of LSO and 'alternative model' firms. The phrase 'rising tides raise all ships' applies. Second, as an emerging market, all parties will have to constantly adjust to new technologies, new entrants, new service models, new process standards, new regulations, and – as one thought leader described it – '*unrelenting cost pressures*'. Third, all parties will have to learn new capabilities, like the disaggregation of work, or significantly improve existing capabilities, like project management. Liam Brown summarised what parties ultimately need to achieve: '*Have the right people, with the right skills, doing the work in the right place.*' Richard Tapp adds to this insight by qualifying that the ultimate client needs to receive '*seamless delivery*' – which might just turn out to be the primary factor shaping the direction of travel of future sourcing models over the longer term.

# Chapter 6

# LSO External Benchmarking: Towards High Performance

## 6.1. Introduction

This chapter is designed to focus attention on what is already being achieved in other business process outsourcing (BPO) areas, and thus underline the potential of alternative sourcing models for legal services. You will see many of the practices we have already identified as useful in legal services, reinforced here. This chapter builds on, extends and gives context to the learning in Chapters 3, 4 and 5, by drawing together the distinctive generic practices we have found across high performance BPO relationships, from whatever sector. As such, it establishes a much needed set of *external benchmarks* for raising performance in the legal services ecosystem.

Chapter 3, you will recall, mapped out 26 practices that emerged from our study of legal service outsourcing stakeholders. These practices are particularly relevant for the stage at which many clients, law firms and service providers now find themselves. In Chapter 4, we made clear that LSO was at an early development stage relative to many other BPO areas, for example, accounting and finance, human resources, back office administration, procurement and estate management. We also mapped the alternative journeys law firms, clients and service providers could be taking in their evolution, and in maturing their capability to leverage external legal services. But a major danger that legal services stakeholders face is in taking an insular, sectoral view on the use of the external market. We have witnessed this all too often in the last 20 years, whether the sectors be, for example, banking, retail, insurance, manufacturing, government or telecommunications. The inclination is to compare yourself with your peers, whether it be fellow banks, insurance companies, or in our case law firms and their clients. A much more powerful way to make progress and innovate is to establish benchmarks across sectors. This is already possible when it comes to effective BPO practices due to the considerable amount of robust research that has been accomplished to date. In this chapter we detail the findings from our own recent study of high performance BPO practices[1], and position them collectively as a vital external benchmark for law firms, clients, General Counsels and service providers alike. Three questions clear the ground for what follows:

First, what do we mean by high performance? The research[2] established that a dual criteria test:

- Meets minimum requirements, meaning that the relationship must meet financial objectives, service level objectives, and deliver consistent and predictable service;

- Captures value beyond cost savings, meaning that the relationships attain top-quartile results in self-reported attainment of value beyond cost. The seven potential sources of additional value include: provide flexibility for changing volumes, prepare for changing business conditions, improve the entire process, improve performance in other parts of the organisation, create additional sources of value in the future, deliver business outcomes not originally expected, and increase top-line performance.

Second, how well are BPO arrangements doing, generally? When we panned across all the BPO research, including our own, we saw outsourcing deals falling into four camps, in terms of performance:

1.  Some 20 per cent are 'High' performers, where cost savings are delivered, clients experience high satisfaction levels, the service is managed beyond SLAs as an end-to-end process, and dynamic innovation is achieved.

2.  Some 25 per cent are 'Good' performers, where cost savings are delivered, SLAs met and client satisfaction experienced as 'good'.

3.  A further 40 per cent are 'Doing OK' with marginal cost savings and client satisfaction delivered, and acceptable service.

4.  A bottom 15 per cent are 'Poor' performers, manifesting in low client satisfaction, poor service performance, and no cost savings, or even increased costs.

It is likely that the LSO sector and its constituent deals will take on this performance distribution as it moves into more complex and larger scale deals.

Third, what are the characteristics of high performing outsourcing relationships? Eight attributes emerged very strongly and formed a distinctive set of practices (see Figure 6.1.). These were not sector specific, nor were they particularly related to size of deals or size of client organisations or business function outsourced. In effect we found a relative handful of companies and their outsourcing providers already showing what is realistic and possible, thus creating a compelling picture of high performance BPO – one that is producing greater business value in measurable ways, and one showing what is

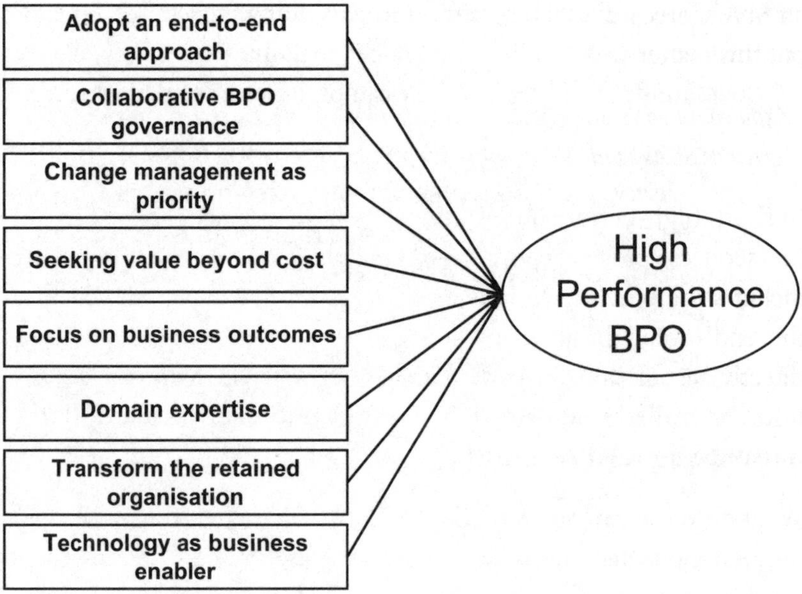

*Figure 6.1: BPO High Performance—Eight Practices*

also possible in the LSO space. This chapter provides insights, research findings and examples for the eight high performance BPO practices. The purpose here is to establish a set of stretch goals, for those contemplating, embarking on, or some way into their legal service outsourcing arrangements.

## 6.2. Practice 1: Adopt an end-to-end approach

What's in scope when it comes to framing the LSO arrangement? In high performance BPO, it is the entire, end-to-end business process, including those elements managed within the client's enterprise, those run by third parties and even other related processes that might have an impact in some way on performance. The client and provider work together to focus on overall process excellence, not simply looking at an SLA scorecard. One executive interviewed as part of our research put this matter well:

> 'You could go to a financial controller in a country and show them a sea of green in SLAs while the process was actually pretty poorly performing.'

In short, high-performance businesses take a more expansive view of the services, processes and functions being outsourced. The client includes the provider and business end-users in the whole picture of the end-to-end business process, even when the provider is only directly accountable for particular sub-processes. The message here – **take a holistic approach to managing the scope of the outsourcing relationship.**

What does it mean, exactly, to take an end-to-end view of a business process? Consider a finance and accounting (F&A) BPO arrangement in which a provider is asked, among other performance SLAs, to post all invoices within three days. A typical BPO performer would focus on hitting that metric. A high performer would look at the matter in a more expansive way. The more important business outcome to be achieved here is to pay that invoice on time and take a discount. But making that happen requires looking at the process end-to-end. When did the invoice get posted and then what happened to it? A provider has to have some sort of impact on the whole cycle time to deliver on the true business outcome indicator that a CFO would care about.

Having better metrics in place to measure process performance is a critical piece of the overall puzzle. High-performance businesses also take the time to look beneath 'average' SLA scores to get to the business outcomes those SLAs are driving toward. One shared services executive spoke to us about the implicit danger of being satisfied with average, because significant under-performance can be hidden in such numbers. In terms of the metric of invoices being paid on time, the company saw an overall 'green' on its performance dashboard. But, said the executive:

> *When you actually broke it down and looked deeper you found a number of refineries had major numbers of trapped invoices — they weren't doing their part of the process properly. So it averaged to a green metric, but it was actually made up of 10 of the businesses doing well and two of them doing not so well.'*

The point is about going beyond the metric and looking more broadly at the process and then at how different areas or units are performing within that overall average metric.

Many of the positive business outcomes delivered from high-performance BPO can be traced in part to this ability to connect the dots around the company as overall process excellence is pursued. As noted by a communications and high-tech company executive:

> *'Outsourcing has certainly driven a much more structured, rigorous and thoughtful planning process. I think traditionally our business was really ad hoc in understanding its needs and planning out how to fulfill those. The outsourcing deal has given us much more structure and, therefore, much more effectiveness.'*

A related point here is that, in high performance BPO, client and provider work together on process consolidation, rationalisation and standardisation across business units and geographies, and this often includes centralisation of services. According to the survey data, 62 per cent of high-performance businesses affirm the importance of process consolidation and standardisation in the BPO relationship compared with only 45 per cent of typical performers. Moreover, 64 per cent of high-performance businesses have successfully implemented more standardised processes compared to just 36 per cent of typical performers.

High-performance BPO also means looking at more than processes in the end-to-end view. It means also looking at people and technology. Half of the high-performance businesses see technology as within the scope of the BPO relationship, while only one-fourth of typical performers agree. The people dimension is the most striking. Almost two-thirds (65 per cent) of high-performance businesses see the impact on people – people from the client and people from the provider – as within the scope of the BPO relationship, compared with only 39 per cent of typical performers. Consider the matter of motivation and engagement of employees: BPO deals are often serviced by a provider's remote delivery teams located in places like India, China, the Philippines and Eastern Europe. Our research has found that providers need clients to acknowledge and reward the provider's staff so they feel connected to their clients. Provider employees appreciate even simple things like a thank-you email or a small token to display in their cubicle. High-performance businesses consider the provider employees an extension of their own teams, including them in events and communications and acknowledging them accordingly.

## 6.3. Practice 2: Collaborative BPO Governance

We found that BPO relationships are starting to separate out according to how well client and provider are moving beyond that 'commodity service' mentality. Is their relationship focused primarily on delivering or consuming a service at a commodity price? Or are they operating together as a cohesive, collaborative team – as strategic partners pursuing not only efficiency but also business outcomes, market opportunities, continuous improvement and higher levels of business value? This commitment to partnering attitudes as a characteristic of high-performance BPO is one of the more striking findings from our research. Nearly 85 per cent of high-performance businesses consider their BPO provider to be a strategic partner; by contrast, only 41 per cent of typical performers operate according to that mindset. The message here – **adopt a partnership attitude.** This message has already surfaced from LSO research as discussed in Chapters 3 and 5. This message fits, and goes beyond Practices 19 and 20 in Chapter 3 – direct in-house lawyers to nurture the LSO provider's lawyers; and have joint and frequent communications with the client, external legal counsel, the LSO provider and, if relevant, the technology provider. It takes much further the stipulation of Practice 24 in Chapter 3 – treat the LSO provider as a partner, not a vendor.

Ironically, a sticking point in moving to more collaborative relationships may, in fact, be one of the very best practices outsourcers are taught to work on: governance structures, including boards, operating committees, management meetings, escalation ladders and executive decision trees. Certainly these are essential to effective management of working processes and contractual agreements. However, by themselves they do not produce high performance. Indeed, if seen as the only component affecting the business relationship, they may even inhibit the kinds of interactions that can drive better business outcomes.

In the high-performance BPO relationships that we studied, collaborative BPO governance is much more than a set of committees or a schedule of meetings; it also comprises the attitudes toward the relationship and the behaviours that strengthen it and drive both parties toward higher levels of performance.

**Collaborative Attitudes.** Client executives in high performance BPO relationships hold deeply the partnership view and actively promote that view among their teams. By example, the client commercial director for a resources company told us:

*'I'm not interested in being a recipient of service. I want us to be strategic partners. It is a word that is tossed around in a clichéd way. But for me, strategic partner means: let's talk about my five most important objectives and how that overlaps with the things that the provider does.'*

**Collaborative Behaviours.** The partnership view is then reinforced through behaviours of individuals but also of the client company as a whole. That is, in high-performance BPO relationships, partnership is not simply a slogan on a poster or inserted into a corporate values report. It is insisted upon by executives with the power to shape the culture of their companies. When client employees lapse into complaining or blaming the provider, the client executives from high-performance relationships will immediately and invariably reaffirm the desired attitudes of the partnership view. Client executives committed to the partnership view may even replace their own employees when they cannot or do not embrace that partnership attitude. We also found a number of other distinctive collaborative behaviours that occurred more frequently in high performance BPO relationships. These include:

- Senior leadership from both parties collaborate to understand each other's objectives. In our survey, 73 per cent of high performance businesses stated that senior leaders from both client and provider spend time to understand each other's objectives and strategies. This was true for only 35 per cent of typical performers.

- Senior leadership from both parties proactively refine objectives as the BPO relationship matures. Among 60 per cent of high-performance businesses, business users receiving services have a high degree of influence in setting the direction of the BPO relationship; only 30 per cent of typical performers noted this capability. The role of the corporate strategy team in refining objectives is also important. Among high-performance businesses, 61 per cent agree that their corporate strategy team has a high degree of influence in setting the direction of the BPO relationship, compared with only 37 per cent of typical performers.

- **Senior leadership from both parties resolve conflicts fairly.** This fits well with our finding from the LSO research in Chapter 3, recorded in Practice 25: resolve issues and conflicts together. One of the largest disparities in BPO performance came from the area of conflict resolution. Fully 90 per cent of high-performance businesses felt that client and provider were able to productively resolve conflicts. This was true only with 44 per cent of typical performers. This is not only a matter of resolving tensions, as important as that certainly is. It is also a matter of seeing conflicts, issues or under-performance as a sign that something is not right in the terms of the agreement or in the relationship itself – and that solving that issue is in the interest of both parties.

- **Companies adapt to changing business and market conditions.** High-performance businesses also work to adapt their BPO arrangement based on changing business or market place conditions such as the challenges companies have faced since the 2008 global economic downturn. In high performance BPO relationships, the provider account executives invariably responded to client requests to help remedy a client's deteriorating commercial position.

Perhaps not surprisingly, contrasting attitudes toward 'partnering' are out there in the BPO world. In typical or low-performing BPO relationships it is not unusual to find that one party will refuse to renegotiate a deal that has turned out to be damaging to the other side. Such executives may say, 'It's not our fault they are losing money, they signed the contract.' Typical quotes from the low performing BPO arrangements we have studied reveal an antagonistic approach to the relationship:

*'They always wait for us [the client] to react to something...they play dead until we kick them' ....'The supplier is only in it to make money.'*

The partnership view is different, both in attitudes and behaviour. As the client executive for one high performer put it:

*'We want them to be successful. No one wants a failing supplier.'*

## 6.4. Practice 3: Change management as priority

BPO changes the way organisations operate. However, the companies we studied differ significantly in their ability to manage that change, both to prevent negative repercussions and to create positive results. The gap between high performers and typical performers is large in terms of attitudes toward change management, but especially when it comes to executing a robust change management programme. Eighty-eight per cent of companies working within a high-performance BPO relationship regard change management as important, compared with 62 per cent of typical performers. And more than three-fourths (77 per cent) of high performance businesses characterise themselves as successful at executing change management plans – 33 percentage points higher than typical performers.

Change management needs to be considered in terms of two different perspectives. Firstly, there are the immediate issues as an organisation is transitioning from its previous mode of operation to the new outsourcing environment. Secondly, in terms of being able to adapt to change in the long run. In the area of transition, our research and interviews found that the ability of a provider to come to the table with experience backed by proven transition methodologies is critically important to effective execution of change management programmes.

Beyond the transition period, change management is also important in driving the outsourcing relationship toward greater levels of value. This was seen in several ways in the research data. For example, nearly 85 per cent of high-performance businesses proactively refine their objectives as the relationship matures compared to just 40 per cent of typical performers. It's a living relationship, evolving to meet a client's ongoing business needs and opportunities in an ever-changing market environment. With the BPO relationship continuously attuned to what the business is doing, what companies are actually doing is creating an organisation that is 'change capable'. That is, companies can no longer afford to think about organisational change as something separate from everything else they do. Change management must be an internal and ever-present capability, which enables the client to achieve more organisational and strategic agility. The message here – **manage the effects of change during transition and beyond.** In the context of LSO, these practices are clearly evident as contributing to positive LSO outcomes. In Chapter 3, clients and providers from successful LSO relationships cited a number of stakeholder buy-ins, and transition of work practices.

Some of the keys to building this internal change capability from BPO research include:

**Seek out and then nurture transformational leaders.** This fits with but goes beyond Practice 15 in Chapter 3 – assign a high-level point person to manage the LSO provider relationship. Managing change requires specific kinds of leadership attitudes and behaviours. Based in part on knowledge of the specific competencies needed to manage change, companies must have dedicated programmes in place to develop the right leadership behaviours, and then provide the appropriate incentives. Transformational leadership is especially important in keeping a BPO relationship energised to create higher levels of value. By way of example, one senior client executive described the new service provider lead in this way:

*'She's fantastic. She's very action-oriented. She pushes back and can challenge us in the right way. That's the difference I think in terms of making it a more strategic approach rather than sitting back and accepting business as usual.'*

However, one of our enduring findings is the importance of leadership pairs in outsourcing relationships. In high performers both client and supplier have transformational leaders who typically exhibit the following attributes and behaviours:[3]

- Individually strong

- Focus on the future

- Spirit of togetherness

- Transparency

- Problem solving

- Outcomes and client first

- Trustworthy/trusting

- Strong chemistry

- Build strong teams

**Stay on target.** Companies need to align with business goals in an ongoing manner, which requires effective project management as well as good governance, including status reporting and issue escalation to business stakeholders.

**Measure your progress.** Metrics are a critical part of any change management programme. There are tools, for example, that can help companies assess the effectiveness of teams and work groups: the pace of change they are experiencing, whether or not they are developing needed skills in sufficient numbers, the effectiveness of work processes and so forth.

## 6.5. Practice 4: Seeking value beyond cost

An executive from a grocery retailer summarised this high-performance BPO practice extremely well in characterising the goals of his BPO initiative. While cost was an important consideration in provider selection, he said, the ability to improve performance was the company's main objective:

> *'Outsourcing was more about service to our customers than about cost reduction. The outsourcing model is obviously woven potentially to save us money, but it wasn't our prime motivation.'*

The message here – **focus on benefits beyond cost reduction.** Of course we met this already for LSO as Practice 3 in Chapter 3. The BPO high performers, however, extract a lot more business value from their outsourcing relationships than we are seeing currently in the LSO space.

This mindset manifests itself first in how the business case for the BPO programme is constructed. Two thirds of high-performance businesses focus on the potential value of business benefits beyond cost alone when creating the business case, compared with only 26 per cent of typical performers. That is, high performers consider cost benefits to be just table stakes.

Moreover, considerably more typical performers focus on low cost of service. Sixty-two per cent of typical performers consider low cost of service to be among their top three sources of value compared to 46 per cent of high performance businesses, who seek other benefits as well. High-performance businesses are also more willing to consider greater functionality from the outsourced service *even if it costs more*. Fifty-eight per cent of high-performance businesses will consider service options with greater value, even at higher costs, compared with 31 per cent of typical performers. The insight here is that cost reduction is great but, by itself, is not a sustainable benefit. High-performance businesses appear to be more driven by the fact that outsourcing can create an organisation capable of greater things. As articulated by the shared service manager for a manufacturing company:

*'You need to know what you are trying to accomplish with outsourcing. You have to be thinking way beyond cost because that is only a one-time gain. Arbitrage is a one-time gain. You want to be thinking about what you will do in your own company and what you will not be doing. Strategy emerges from that.'*

## 6.6. Practice 5: Focus on business outcomes

As just discussed, effective BPO relationships go beyond focusing only on cost issues to pursue higher levels of business value. This fits with Practice 13 in Chapter 3 – use Key Performance Indicators (KPIs) to incent adoption by in-house lawyers. But beyond that, they aim for specific strategic outcomes that can be measured and that can help achieve competitive advantage. And then, beyond even that, they forge deals such that an outsourcing provider commits to the achievement of those outcomes – paying a penalty if they are not met or sharing in rewards if they are. We met this practice to a degree in Chapter 3 with Practice 8: mandate yearly productivity improvements. But BPO high performers go considerably beyond this. In our survey, 62 per cent of high performance businesses consider business impact targets as an important component of the BPO service model, compared with 50 per cent of typical performers. High performers see more potential from the relationship to achieve greater ends: 56 per cent are looking to achieve competitive advantage through BPO, while only 28 per cent of typical performers aim for that goal. The message here – **target strategic business outcomes, not just more efficient transactions.**

Part of the answer here is to look beyond SLA performance. Certainly, excellence in service delivery is a characteristic of high-performance BPO, but partners in these relationships also look beyond, to innovations and better business performance. In some cases this means re-examining SLAs so they support the attainment of timely business goals. An executive with one provider notes that the client-provider team is not content with merely meeting SLAs but instead continues to re-examine the SLAs in light of the business outcomes they are intended to produce. The ultimate purpose is to resolve service requests and issues rather than simply meet an SLA to answer phones or respond to emails in a given time period. Said one provider executive:

*'We have a responsibility to deliver to our contractual obligations, and that includes meeting SLAs, which are targeted at being efficient. However, we also put emphasis on making sure we drive the right end-to-end results, making sure things are better for the client, meaning we target being effective.'*

Thus, the partners work to refine SLAs in light of those dual goals. Innovation is often mentioned rhetorically when establishing a BPO relationship, but how, exactly, do client and provider put in place the structures and measures to make innovation happen? And, equally important, who pays? Providers may be reluctant to spend time and expert resources on an ancillary part of the contract, especially when clients themselves do not take the positive actions required to work with the provider to drive innovation. The other sticking point when it comes to driving more strategic outcomes has to do with motivation. Clients in high performance BPO relationships understand that they need to incent providers if they expect to achieve higher-impact or even transformative results. For a significant number of high-performance businesses, the answer is outcome-based pricing.

One form of such arrangement which is higher up the maturity curve is a contract in which performance incentives are built into it. More than half of high performers (54 per cent) have such incentives in place, compared with only about one-fourth (24 per cent) of typical performers. Not quite as mature, but beginning to come into its own, is a gain-sharing arrangement, in which a provider agrees to drive improved performance in a particular area of the client's company in exchange for a share of the additional business value created. The gap between high-performance businesses and typical performance in this area is already significant, with 39 per cent of high-performance businesses operating under a gain-sharing agreement, compared with just 16 per cent of typical engagements. Such an arrangement can be advantageous for both parties, and fits with Practice 10 in Chapter 3 – gain-share the benefits from specific innovation projects.

A significant challenge in gain-sharing, however, is figuring out the actual benefits to share fairly as gains. In real business contexts, many external factors can influence performance outcomes. How can the partners isolate the effects of a single innovation project? One client and provider approach this issue by agreeing to the gain-share in advance. They created a transformation programme with an associated governance structure to embed innovations and transformation projects into the relationship from the start. This gels to some extent with Practice 9 in Chapter 3 – dedicate time each year to drive the innovation agenda, but again high performers go beyond even that. The partners effectively answered the question: 'Who will pay the up-front investments for innovations?' Innovations are delivered via transformation projects, and are funded by the client from the savings generated by outsourcing. Funding for innovation is driven by a programme that is outside of the economics of the original contract. This implies that the client compensates the supplier for any impact the innovation would have on their original contract economics. They align incentives through gain-sharing, but avoid potential disagreements by agreeing to the gain-share specifics in advance.

## 6.7. Practice 6: Domain expertise and analytics

As BPO evolves, matures, and enables richer and more complex business outcomes – the field of providers is beginning to separate out in terms of their ability to provide new levels of value. In earlier generations of BPO, the focus was primarily on greater efficiency: standardising and streamlining operations, running a business function better and faster, and driving out cost wherever possible. But companies can pull the same levers of labour savings and process improvements for only so long before the benefits begin to sound less impressive. Now, the legitimate question clients are asking of their outsourcing providers, including in the LSO space, is, 'Is there something else you can give me?' That 'something else' turns out to be the ability to use deep domain and industry knowledge and the ability to analyse data about the functions and processes being outsourced – to more predictably drive business outcomes, as just discussed. Both industry and process expertise are important to today's outsourcing clients. *The message here* – **contextualise data through domain expertise and analytics.**

From our survey, almost half (48 per cent) of high-performance businesses consider their provider's industry experience to be important, compared with only 31 per cent of typical performers. Process expertise is important to two-thirds (67 per cent) of high-performance businesses, but only 48 per cent of the others. Even more important, however, is what providers do with that industry knowledge on behalf of their clients. Outsourcing providers are uniquely positioned with sight lines across entire industries as well as across their clients' operations, including customers, global supply chains, business units and decision-making structures. Providers accumulate a wealth of data and information as they run business processes or IT services for a client over the course of a multi-year contract. If providers have a mature analytics capability, they can deploy that capability to measure the right key process indicators, tools and techniques to measure and report on KPIs and deployed algorithms, models and sophisticated statistics to identify weaknesses and opportunities, and then redesign processes to deliver measurable business outcomes.

In high-performance BPO, clients know how important their provider's analytics capability is to achieving greater business value. Forty-two per cent of high performers consider analytics provided by their service provider as an important priority in the BPO relationship, compared with 28 per cent of typical performers. Almost half of the high performers surveyed (48 per cent) acknowledge the importance of using data and information to capture additional benefits, compared with only one-fourth of typical performers.

Two additional points are important to make. First, companies should develop a mindset that is attuned to the multiple cause-and-effect loops of their organisation, so they know what to do with data about the performance of a function. To take one basic example, a spike in customer inquiries to a call centre needs to trigger a response different than simply improving capacity or increasing efficiency in the call centre. It means something is wrong elsewhere in the product supply chain – perhaps manufacturing or delivery. Effective 'organisational diagnosticians' are essential when it comes to analytics. Just as medical doctors know that a pain in one part of the body might signal trouble somewhere else, so it is with organisational performance.

Second, what's perhaps most important in this high-performance BPO practice is the manner in which domain expertise and analytics become an iterative cycle that makes both the client and provider stronger. Domain expertise enables the companies to identify contexts and scenarios in which data analytics might produce insight; those insights in turn cycle back to increase understanding of the company and its industry. This cycle creates a kind of relentless drive toward improvement and innovation that is difficult to replicate in companies not availing themselves of advanced analytics capabilities.

But this cycle cannot be sustained unless a level of trust is attained such that the client allows the provider very close contact with company strategy and data. As one provider account executive said, the biggest key to success in delivering advantage from analytics is:

> *'Understanding the client's business – using their business outcomes to create the right delivery model for them. It is absolutely critical to know what their objectives are. [So the issue is getting access to their] executive-level people and using those objectives to create the right delivery model and set performance levels for our team supporting them.'*

## 6.8. **Practice 7: Transformation of the retained organisation**

Transitioning to a BPO relationship can be tough on workers in the retained organisation if steps are not taken to help them succeed in the new environment. Their roles will often shift and they will find themselves charged with managing and co-ordinating the outsourcing service relationship rather than simply managing others executing tasks. There may also be cultural differences between the retained and outsourced workforce which need to be dealt with carefully. Aligning the organisation's corporate culture with new ways of working and integrating the culture of the outsourced workforce is important. Ultimately, what a company seeks is a 'one team' mentality across all workforces and the alignment of all workforces into an integrated and unified organisational structure. So it is perhaps not surprising, then, that our research found that high-performance businesses place as much importance on internal transformation as they place on transforming the outsourced processes. More than world-class outsourced processes are needed; companies also need to transform the retained organisation that is responsible for managing the service and clarify roles, responsibilities and requisite skills. Our survey found that half of high-performance businesses have engaged in modifications of their retained organisation to optimise the BPO operating model, compared with only 29 per cent of typical performers. The message here – **enable the retained organisation to perform effectively in the new environment.**

An essential part of the retained organisation transformation takes us back to some of the change management methods and principles discussed earlier. As the global procurement process manager for a fragrance and flavours company put it:

*'All the change management is absolutely critical. You never have enough communication and meetings with each side and with each stakeholder, explaining why we are doing it, what we are going to change, why we are changing, what the escalation procedures are, and so forth. They can't stop talking with the counterpart in the BPO before they escalate to the president of purchasing. This kind of element of work is very important in the day-to-day operations of the BPO arrangement.'*

In addition to the change management programme put in place, three additional streams of work need to happen to enable the transformation of the retained organisation:

- Aligning organisational structures and operating models – organisation architecture and design; job realignment and performance management.

- Enhancing skills and capabilities of the retained workforce – training, knowledge transfer and performance support.

- Maximising co-ordination and interaction between the retained and outsourced workforces – organisational culture, cross-cultural awareness and workforce collaboration.

This approach is clearly helping many of the clients with whom we spoke. A procurement process manager told us:

*'We really involved the current, in-house purchasing organisation into the process as much as possible so they felt they had ownership of the transformation.'*

This manager also highlighted an additional key to success: baseline the performance of the 'old' way of working so that fair comparisons can be made to performance under a BPO relationship:

*'Otherwise, when the BPO starts working, people only notice what's going worse than before, not necessarily when it is getting better. Also, they tend to have a very rosy vision of how their life was in the past. So having a few baseline surveys or a similar kind of data point is quite useful when it comes to showing if we are making progress or not making progress, with facts rather than perceptions.'*

## 6.9. Practice 8: Technology as business enabler

In high-performance BPO relationships, technology is more than just the 'plumbing' of the BPO solution; it is a source of innovation and advantage. Savvy clients look for differentiated technology capabilities from their providers. For example, 40 per cent of high performance businesses consider technology provided by the service provider to be an important component of the BPO relationship, compared to only 27 per cent of typical performers. Even greater numbers of high performers, 56 per cent, believe it is important to gain access to technology in a BPO relationship, while only 34 per cent of typical performers agree. The message here – **use technology to drive operational improvements and business innovation.**

One of the value-added aspects of technology has already been noted: the analytics capabilities integrated into the services of a BPO provider. For example, one supplier developed a tool to improve BPO performance through analytics and benchmarking. It provides a central portal with real-time visibility into a client's business performance, including operational and contractual metrics and analytics. The tool incorporates performance benchmarking data from multiple BPO relationships, enabling a rich source of information with which to 'navigate' toward higher levels of value. Technology can also support a BPO relationship through better forecasting. As the executive for a manufacturing company explained:

*'The provider has worked with its own proprietary tools to forecast the demand in different regions of the world and recommended some relocation of material in different regions so we meet the demands more properly, it then validated that the supply chain was delivered accordingly. We ended up with enough parts supplied to support them. As a result, we've yielded, for the first time, service levels with a first fill rate above 90 per cent.'*

Effective technologies and architectures contribute to cost reductions and more efficient operations by streamlining the systems environment and reducing the number of systems involved, often standardising the technology environment on a unified, centralised platform. As one client explained, technology innovation is another advantage of a high-performance BPO arrangement:

*'The provider has brought in a group of small but effective proprietary tools that they have but we would never develop, which is the advantage of outsourcing. For example, they have a piece of software which is now resident on our system which checks for duplications. They also offered us a service in going back before implementation and checking for duplications of vendor invoices – have we paid the same invoice twice? They have another one which sets up a vendor portal which allows the supplier to see a picture of his account with us. So instead of ringing us and saying, where's my invoice, he can see what the progress is. None of these are fantastically huge systems but there's a whole set of little programmatic tools that they bring to bear which has been very useful for us in our aim of going back to the beginning and improving the process.'*

In our research into high performing outsourcing relationships we also found technology-based tools providing effective monitoring of performance, and also creating the kind of transparency of information that can foster trust between client and providers. Furthermore, high-performance BPO relationships commit to exploring how current technology trends can be applied to improving operational performance. A distinct advantage of technology in a BPO relationship is that it can drive a one-to-many model of standardised processes and technologies so that clients achieve greater efficiencies from their providers. Beyond that, other emerging technologies such as cloud computing will help drive innovations in future generations of BPO. Providers should be considering, where appropriate, moving aspects of technology infrastructure onto a hosted, on-demand platform. There are trade-offs with such a strategy particularly when a provider has the sophistication to create a hybrid model involving on-premises and hosted solutions, cloud can provide cost and flexibility benefits that are hard to beat. Updates can be made to the software and new configurations and capabilities can be implemented through the cloud configuration.

## 6.10. Conclusion

Until recently, companies were looking for something relatively straightforward from a BPO relationship: greater efficiency, streamlined operations and lower costs. Currently in the LSO space, those attracted or pressured into external sourcing are learning to look for more. But today, in the broader BPO market, companies expect much more: business insight, innovation, industry expertise, solutions adapted to more individualised needs, a commitment to continuous improvement, supplier partnering and commitment to strategic business outcomes. That is, the broader BPO industry today is moving to a 'cost-plus-value' proposition focused on delivering business, even strategic business impact, not just operating cost reductions. But what exactly is the 'value' in that proposition? And how do the best-performing BPO relationships go about achieving that value? What separates them from the rest? And what can legal clients, General Counsels, legal service providers and other stakeholders learn from these broader BPO experiences?

In this chapter we spelt out the attributes of 'high performance BPO' – BPO that produces business value for a company that exceeds that of its industry peers in a way that can be sustained over time. The challenge is for legal service stakeholders to compare their sourcing practices, behaviours and performances not just against their legal service peers, but against external benchmarks derived from what is going on in the broader BPO space. The results could bring both unpleasant and pleasant surprises, but, in both cases, hopefully accelerated learning will take place. Looking across what is distinctive about BPO high performers, one thing is quite striking: the extent to which they have moved on from outsourcing administration and contract management issues and a focus on cost and service trade-offs, to relationship management and strategic outcomes, and raising the performance game continuously. This maturing is reflected also in the distinctive, intense focus on getting the soft areas of management right. Partnering and collaboration, transformational leadership, change management, retained skills and capabilities seem to be prime drivers of achieving superior business outcomes through using the external services market. We see legal services needing to get the basics right on outsourcing then moving more rapidly in this direction, if it is to truly leverage what is currently available and the potential value inherent in the global legal services marketplace. We conclude the book in the next chapter with seven research informed predictions on how things are likely to unfold.

---

1    See Mindrum, C., Hindle, J., Lacity, M., Simonson, E., Sutherland, C., and Willcocks, L. (2012), 'Achieving High Performance in BPO: Research Report', Accenture. Each of the eight practices is described in its own detailed report available from www.outsourcingunit.com and www.Accenture.com websites. Here we supply a summary, as these practices relate to LSO development.

2    The research consisted of several streams. These included a quantitative survey of 263 buyer executives, in-depth interviews with client-provider executive pairs in more than 20 organisations, research into 26 organisations identified as high-performance businesses in collaborative innovation, and a review of 1,356 BPO and ITO findings from 254 academic

research studies. The research was carried out on behalf of Accenture by Everest Group and The Outsourcing Unit at the London School of Economics. Survey respondents were all at senior or C-levels, and their companies included a wide range of organisations, with 40 per cent being from companies with revenues exceeding $10 billion annually. A broad distribution of types of BPO was included in the survey.

3   See Lacity, M. And Willcocks, L. (2013), 'Outsourcing Business Process For Innovation'. *Sloan Management Review,* 54, (3), *pp. 63–70.*

# Chapter 7

# LSO Market Predictions

## 7.1. Introduction

We have been studying ITO since 1989 and BPO since 2000. Before these markets matured, potential clients voiced similar concerns with ITO and BPO that we now hear pertaining to LSO. These concerns include 'This work is core to my business; it's too strategic to outsource.' 'How can I trust a provider with my data and intellectual property?' 'Our work is specialised – how can providers possibly do what we do?' 'Isn't it a pain to work with offshore providers?' As the markets for ITO and BPO matured, clients learned how to engage outsourcing providers in ways that delivered business results and addressed these concerns. The paths to maturity for the ITO and BPO markets were surprisingly similar, and based on our deep understanding of those markets, we foresee LSO following a similar path to maturity. We predict:

1. The shape of enterprise legal functions will increasingly move from 'pyramids' to 'diamonds'.

2. Enterprise legal functions will conduct more panel reviews, reduce the number of law firm partners and increase bundled legal services.

3. Law firms will respond.

4. LSO providers will move up the value chain.

5. New engagement models will emerge.

6. Significant M&A and strategic alliance activity will fuel provider growth and capabilities.

7. New locations will become competitive.

8. Technology will play an increasing role in the provision of legal services.

## 7.2. **Transforming the shape of enterprise legal functions from pyramids to diamonds**

We've identified the shape-shift of back office functions from 'pyramids' to 'diamonds' as a major trend in IT, Finance, Accounting, Indirect Procurement, and Human Resources functions[1] (see Figure 7.1). We predict that a similar transformation will occur in enterprise legal functions.

Pyramids are heavily populated with employees, most of whom are at the bottom of the pyramid. The benefit of this design is that employees continually build valuable, client-specific experience as they are promoted higher up the pyramid. The pyramid model is strong on retained knowledge, but it is also costly. Back office managers trying to recruit college graduates must compete with providers (or law firms in the case of enterprise legal functions) who can court them with far richer career paths and many more peers. The model also tends to rely on staff augmentation with expensive domestic workers (law firms in the case of legal services) to fill in skills gaps and to scale up resources. The pyramid model is also characterised by a significant class of middle managers who manage both employees and supplemental staff.

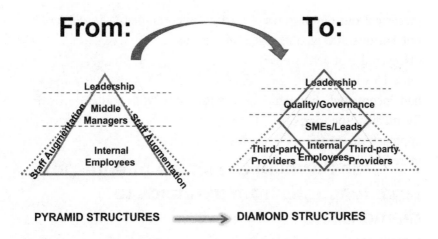

*Figure 7.1: Changing Shape of Back Office Functions*[2]

Diamond-shaped retained organisations replace the heavy bottom of the pyramid with providers. Many transactional activities that were once performed by employees are performed now by providers, typically in a lower cost location. There are fewer middle managers, but more Subject Matter Experts (SMEs) and Project Leads. The diamond-shaped organisation also needs more quality assurance and governance skills to co-ordinate services with providers. The benefits of the diamond-shaped retained organisation are lower costs, access to providers with best-of-breed skills, and greater flexibility because providers can more easily adapt to increases or decreases in service volumes. It does not require a stretch of the imagination to see how the diamond model can also transform enterprise legal functions and perhaps even the traditional structure of law firms.[3]

## 7.3. **More panel reviews and bundled services**

In the ITO and BPO markets, many clients initially pursued an ad hoc approach to outsourcing, with decentralised units engaging in piecemeal outsourcing, resulting in a large number of providers. In one Fortune 500 manufacturing firm, for example, the corporate CIO discovered that across business units, the company had engagements with 15 offshore ITO providers. Furthermore, three different units had negotiated different rates with the same Indian provider! Eventually, the corporate CIO took a more strategic, proactive approach to outsourcing, reduced the number of providers, and increased the bundling of services. We saw many other organisations consolidating from many providers to bundled ITO and BPO services.[4] We predict a similar trend will occur in enterprise legal functions.[5] In 2012, for example, Atos completely transformed and centralised their in-house legal function and for the first time appointed a select panel of global law firms, which included LPO provider UnitedLex.[6]

Many enterprise legal functions engage multiple law firms, each specialising in a different legal area. The transaction costs of managing multiple firms are high, and several large companies are already reducing the number of legal providers or packaging legal work and tendering it out to the lowest bidder.[7] At Colt Technology Services, for example, the Legal Chief told *The Lawyer*: *'I think we probably have too many firms; The name of the game is building stronger relationships with fewer firms.'*[8] In June 2010, Microsoft engaged Wipro to provide patent and trademark services. Previously Microsoft used in-house resources, outside law firms and offshore vendors to provide IP services. Moving to Wipro *'ensured not only efficiency but also consistency in the way Microsoft does business.'*[9]

## 7.4. Law firms will respond

We recognise that many law firms are threatened by LSO providers because the LSO model can cannibalise law firm revenues and portend the demise of the lucrative pyramid structure. While some studies show that 77 per cent of private law firms in the UK have not considered any response to LSO, 23 per cent have responded with alternative solutions.[10] Some law firms have set up captive centres onshore, nearshore, and/or offshore to help reduce costs, which are passed to clients in the form of lower fees. Other law firms have partnered with LSO providers, and their innovative sourcing approach has helped to secure new business from cost-conscious clients. In reality, the law firms comprise most of the value of legal services market. In the US, for example, 80 per cent of the legal spend is generated from law firms and 20 per cent from in-house counsel. Thus the opportunities afforded by global LSO provision should in theory be most relevant for law firms. If law firms are willing to understand how LSO providers can actually strengthen their capabilities in terms of superior technology, process standardisation, and even better project management from some full service LSO providers, then the forces of globalisation may create value for all three parties – clients, LSO providers and law firms.

## 7.5. LSO providers will move up the value chain

Like ITO and BPO, the initial driver of LSO has been lower costs available through labour arbitrage. Clients initially feel most comfortable sending discrete work with low complexity and low criticality offshore, the so called 'white chip' work. (In poker, tradition has it that white chips are the least valuable, red chips are of medium value, and blue chips are most valuable[11]) (see Figure 7.2). If LSO follows a path similar to ITO and BPO growth, the LSO market will move up the value chain to include more red chip and even blue chip work. Client organisations will increasingly source work that has medium complexity and medium criticality ('red chip' work) to major law firms, to offshore LSO providers via major law firms, or to offshore LSO providers directly. Client organisations will continue to use their own in-house counsel (insourcing) for high-value work that is highly complex and highly critical ('blue chip' work), but some clients will engage in strategic partnerships with major law firms or LSO providers to perform such work. Strategic partnerships are appropriate for 'blue chip' work when clients and providers can identify a mutually beneficial engagement that fosters innovation and trust and when the partners can align incentives and share risks and rewards. And as clients and providers build long-term relationships based on trust, transparency, and collaboration, clients will likely engage providers for more end-to-end solutions.

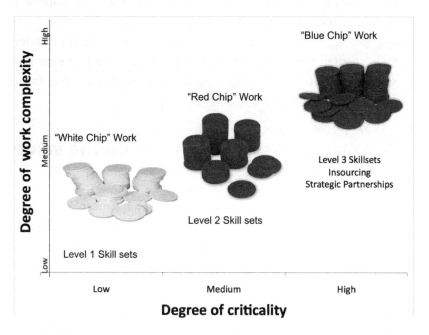

*Figure 7.2: LSO Work as a Function of Complexity and Criticality*[12]

## 7.6. New engagement models will emerge

Besides moving up the value chain, enterprise legal functions will likely find many new ways to engage LSO providers. Currently, many enterprise legal functions engage offshore LSO providers directly, or they access offshore LSO services indirectly from their major law firms. The first engagement model requires more hands-on management, but the benefit is that the enterprise legal function retains all the cost benefits. The second engagement model is a subcontracting model that places management oversight with a major law firm. Presumably major law firms have, or will soon gain core capabilities in managing offshore LSO providers since they can reap advantages from replicating the model over many clients. As for pricing models, initially clients used a supplemental staffing model based on fee per unit of time. As engagements get longer, clients and providers may move increasingly away from supplemental staffing models to managed services (see Figure 7.3).

If LSO follows the path of ITO and BPO, we may see even more strategic engagement models emerge, like gainsharing models that align client-provider objectives and incent innovation[13] or like the enterprise partnership model we've studied between Xchanging and BAE Systems and Lloyd's of London.[14] The enterprise partnership is an engagement model in which a client and provider create a jointly owned enterprise that both services the client investor as well as seeks external customers. However, this is not a traditional joint venture with equally shared risks and rewards. Rather, the provider bears more risk and the primary purpose of the enterprise is to transform the client investor's back office. The enterprise partnership addresses the lack of alignment in fee-for-service outsourcing while minimising the client risks of a joint venture.

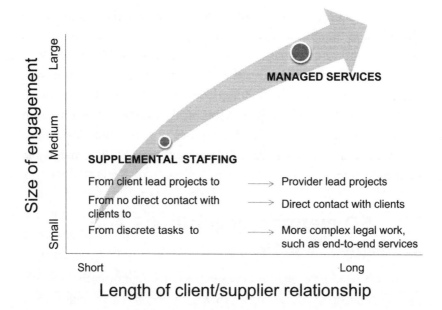

*Figure 7.3: From Supplemental Staffing to Managed Services*[12]

With regard to how the law firms will engage with their clients, the pressure is mounting to move from the classic hourly rate to a fixed fee. Clients' expectations, fuelled by their experiences with ITO and BPO, are that fixed fees should be applicable for legal work the majority of the time. To us, this seems to be at the foundations of many of the shifts we are seeing in the market at the moment. Most of the new innovative providers (for example: Riverview Law, Keystone Law, radiant.law) all offer fixed fee work as the default option. Until that becomes more common, particularly amongst the established firms, the traditional providers will prevail.

Following the Legal Services Act 2007 in the UK, which, amongst other things, allows non-lawyers to own legal firms, an increasing number of Alternative Business Structures (ABSs) are being created. Although this aspect is still fairly specific to the UK and a number of other jurisdictions, it is bound to spread around the world. Some sizeable and significant organisations, such as the Co-Op (a high street retailer), BT (a telecoms provider) and the RAC (a motoring organisation), have created their own law firms to service their customers' specific needs. Building the capability within a non-legal organisation to provide legal services will create additional demand for outsourced legal services and, conversely, some of these new ABSs could spin out of their parent companies to become LSO providers in their own right.

## 7.7. LSO mergers, acquisitions, and strategic alliances

As the ITO and BPO markets matured, we saw that growth for larger providers occurred inorganically, that is, by mergers and acquisitions. Inorganic growth has many benefits including rapid market expansion, improved suite of services, elimination of competition, lower operating costs, and access to human and intellectual capital.[15] Some of the biggest M&A deals in ITO – the most mature outsourcing market for services – actually occurred within the last five years; Hewlett-Packard (HP) acquired Electronic Data Systems (EDS) in 2008 for about $14 billion. Xerox acquired Affiliated Computer Services (ACS) in 2009 for about $7.4 billion. Dell acquired Perot Systems in 2009 for $3.9 billion.

The LSO space has already seen increased M&A activity, and we predict this trend will continue. Notable acquisitions in the LSO space include Thomson Reuters' acquisition of Pangea3 in 2010 for $35 to $40 million, UnitedLex's acquisition of LawScribe in 2010, and several acquisitions by Integreon, including Datum Legal in 2008, ONSIGHT3 in 2009, and an investment of $50 million from Actis in 2010.[16] More recently, UnitedLex bought Crownbridge Group LLC, which is based in Atlanta and has offices in Hyderabad.[17] And in one of the biggest deals announced thus far, UK-based Cinven Partners announced its acquisition of CPA Global for $1.45 billion in February of 2012.[18]

The number of strategic alliances will also increase, an early example being the 2010 alliance between IDS Legal and H3 Consulting that provides corporate law departments and law firms with litigation and regulatory document discovery services.[19] In June of 2010, Satyam announced a partnership with Direct Channel Holdings, one of Africa's leading BPO companies.[20] LSO services are just one of the many services offered by Satyam.

## 7.8. New locations will become competitive

As noted in Chapters 1 and 2, India and the Philippines are the top offshore destinations for LSO services. These two countries have strong capabilities in terms of higher education, English-language competence, process and IT maturity, and deep expertise in providing IT and BP services to Western-based clients. Both of these countries continue to build LSO capabilities, with new providers and captive centres[21] announced monthly. India is also seeking assistance from US law school teachers to update curriculum across India's 900 law schools.[22]

In the ITO and BPO markets, BRIC countries (Brazil, Russia, India, and China) initially created the offshore market, but soon after many countries found unique competitive positions within the global playing field. Eastern European countries like Poland and the Czech Republic offered multi-lingual skills and European Union membership advantages. North Africa also offered Europe and the Middle East cost, language, and time zone advantages. Niche markets in Costa

Rica, Chile, and other Central and South American countries offered North American clients Spanish language capabilities, lower costs, and favorable time zones.

In the LSO market, Scotland, Ireland, and South Africa look particularly primed to compete with India and the Philippines. Scotland has the advantages of near-shore appeal to the London market and a strong talent pool with nearly 13,000 lawyers.[23] Ireland has a growing base of legal captive centres[24] and about 9,000 qualified lawyers.[25] South Africa increasingly offers Western-based clients cultural compatibility, lower costs, and service excellence in customer support, legal, and financial services.[26] There are over 20,000 qualified lawyers in South Africa.[27]

Our point: we predict that LSO providers will develop on all inhabited continents, serving local, offshore, and even international clients.

## 7.9 Technology will play an increasing role in the provision of legal services

The exploitation of technology has always gone hand-in-hand with outsourcing – even more so with the relatively recent development of cloud services. But this is becoming just as significant with regard to LSO – just look at eDiscovery that blends document review by computer software with a slightly more complex version carried out by humans. Technologies such as Matter Management and IP Management software can help deliver fundamental changes to the way legal departments work, often driving many of the process improvements and efficiencies. GCs wishing to transform their legal departments should be considering their strategy to include technology, processes and sourcing.

Of particular interest in the legal sector is the use of automation software – these are highly intelligent systems that can replace a fair proportion of the basic work currently done by humans (e.g. simple contract drafting) but need no feeding or sleeping, and cost a fraction of the money, even when compared to offshore resources. Thus high volume, repetitive and rule-based processes are ideally suited to automating. The introduction of automation software in wider BPO services is already starting to have a fundamental impact on the BPO business model and the sector overall, and we would expect this to have a similar effect on LSO.

## 7.10. Conclusion

*'In the future, we will do more with LPO. We haven't got a specific target goal in relation to percentage of work, but I do foresee that we'll grow it significantly.'* – General Counsel

*'I think we are going to continue to embed it. Every year we are sending more and more work to the LPO provider.'* – General Counsel

Overall, the General Counsels from the client companies we studied are forward-looking and offered great insights about the future of legal work and the contribution of LSO provision to that future. They are also firmly grounded in the present. They understand that expectations of resistant stakeholders must be actively managed by early and frequent communication and their behaviours must be guided by creating incentives and/or by circumventing, squashing, or co-opting obstructionists. They understand that outsourcing relationships are founded on a sound sourcing strategy, a thorough process for evaluating providers, a realistic business case that balances cost and quality objectives, strong client retained capabilities, sound contracts and strong relational governance.

The providers in our study are equally future-oriented and are actively globalising their firms to best service client needs. Many offer offshore, onshore, and near-shore delivery. Global coverage speeds turnaround times by offering clients multiple shifts, balances the clients' cost and service requirement objectives, and supports multiple languages. But they too are grounded in the present and manage their relationships work order by work order. The Head of Managed Services for one provider summarised the attention to detail on each work order as *'We're maniacal about quality.'*

The clients and providers from this research all foresee that their use of LSO providers will increase in the future. We too are bullish on LSO, but we caution that LSO will likely have its share of failures and disappointments. Even today in the more mature ITO and BPO markets, about 16 per cent of contracts result in failure and about 25 per cent result in no changes in performance as a consequence of outsourcing.[28] Enterprise legal functions and law firms will have to master a number of new capabilities to maximise the chances for successful LSO engagements. We hope that the practices presented here will quicken the learning process.

---

1   See Lacity, M., and Willcocks, L. (2012), 'Mastering High-Performance: Transformation of the Client's Retained Organisation.

2   The figure of the pyramid and diamond was adapted from Jim Lammers of Express Scripts and from Sandy Ogg of Unilver.

3   Lacity, M., and Willcocks, L. (2012), 'Mastering High-Performance: Transformation of the Client's Retained Organisation.

4   See Willcocks, L., Oshri, I., and Hindle, J. (2012), 'Best-of-Breed versus Bundled Services', in Lacity, M., and Willcocks, P., (2012) *Advanced Outsourcing Practice: Rethinking ITO, BPO, and Cloud Services*, Palgrave, London.

5   'The Legal Services Market: The Race is On.' A Report by Espírito Santo's Investment Bank, 2011.

6   'Starting from Scratch', *Legal Week*, Vol. 14, (41), November, 2012, p. 14.

7   Burton, L. (2012), 'Balfour Beatty to Slash Legal Spend by 30 per cent in Panel Review', *The Lawyer*, November , available at www.thelawyer.com

8   From "The In-House Interview: Colt Resolver," *The Lawyer*, 2010.

9   'Wipro Partners with Microsoft to Deliver Global Legal Process Outsourcing Efficiencies', *Business Wire*, June 14, 2010.

10  Griffins, C. (2012), 'LPOver and Out?' *The Lawyer*, October 22, p. 16.

11  From Lacity, M., Rottman, J., and Carmel, E. (2012), 'Emerging ITO and BPO Markets: Rural Sourcing and Impact Sourcing', *IEEE Readynotes*, IEEE Computer Society.

12  Figures 7.2 and 7.3 adapted from Lacity, M., Carmel, E. and Rottman, J. (2011), 'Rural Outsourcing: Delivery ITO and BPO Services from Remote Domestic Locations,' IEEE Computer, Vol. 44, pp. 55–62.

13  Lacity, M., and Willcocks, L. (2012), 'Mastering High-Performance: Dynamic Innovation', working paper.

14  See Willcocks, L., and Lacity, M. (2006), *Global Sourcing of Business and IT Services*, Palgrave, United Kingdom.

15  McHenry, D. and Silva, W. (2010), 'An Acquisition or Organic Growth Strategy?' *PEO Insider*, http://www.silvacapital.com/pdf/silva10.pdf. Last accessed 2012.

16  *The Blackbook of Outsourcing*, 2011, SO00003–004.

17  'UnitedLex Buys Legal Process Outsourcing Firm in Georgia', *M&A Navigator*, May 22, 2012.

18  'CPA Recasts Internal Units Ahead of Sales', *Mint*, February 24, 2012.

19  From 'IDS Legal Names H3 Consulting as West Coast Client Services Provider', *India Business Newsweekly*, 2010, issue 24.

20  'Mahindra Satyam BPO Announces Partnership with Direct Channel Holdings' June 30, 2010. http://www.mahindrasatyam.com/media/pr1june10.asp

21  'Merrill Corporation Adds Legal Process Outsourcing Services to Chennai India', *Business Wire*, March 19, 2012.

22  'Indo-US Ties and the Next Generation of Law Teachers', SSRN Working Paper Series, Rochester, December 2012. http://dx.doi.org/10.2139/ssrn.1702421.

23  Glennie, R. 'The Case for Scotland', *Legal Process Outsourcing Handbook*, available at www.globallegalpost.com; Misra, S., 'An Onshore-Offshore LPO Delivery Model for Europe', *Legal Process Outsourcing Handbook*, available at www.globallegalpost.com

24  Griffins, C. (2012), 'LPOver and Out?' *The Lawyer*, October 22, p. 16.

25  OMC Partners, *Comparative Location Survey for Legal Services Delivery*, November 2011. Available at www.omc-partners.com

26  Willcocks, L. Craig, A., and Lacity, M. (2013), 'Becoming Strategic – South Africa's BPO Service Advantage', The Outsourcing Unit Working Paper Series, available at http://www.outsourcingunit.org/wp.html

27  OMC Partners, *Comparative Location Survey for Legal Services Delivery*, November 2011. Available at www.omc-partners.com

28  See Lacity, M., and Willcocks, P. (2012), *Advanced Outsourcing Practice: Rethinking ITO, BPO, and Cloud Services*, Palgrave, London.

# List of LSO providers

*Please note: The list of LSO providers changes frequently, thus we cannot guarantee the completeness or accuracy of this list.*

Accentia Technologies
Acumen Legal Services
Aeren IT Solutions
American Discovery
Aphelion
Axiom
Bodhi Global
Brigade
Capgemini
CCS
Clairvolex
Clearspire
Clutch
Cobra Legal
Comat Technologies
CPA Global
Dextrasys
Doar
EED
Elevate
Evalueserve
Exactus
Exigent
EXLService

kserve
Lawyers Back Office
Legal Advantage
Legal Professionals India
Legal Source
Legal Support Global Group
LegalEase
Legalwise
Legasis
Lex Global
LEX Outsourcing
Lexadigm
Lexecute
LexHarbor
Lexite Solutions
LexPlosion
Lexquisite
LexSphere
Lotus Legal
Manthan Legal
Merrill Corporation
Mindcrest
NewGalexy
Novus Law

| | |
|---|---|
| Firstsource | Offshore Services to Lawyers |
| Fox Mandal | Outside Counsel |
| Fusion Legal Services | Pangea3 |
| Gausa | Patni |
| Genpact | Power Legal |
| GVK Bio | Quatrro |
| HCL | QuisLex |
| IBM (Daksh) | Reverse Informatics |
| iBridge | SDD Global Solutions |
| iDiligence | SPi |
| IDS Legal | Talwar & Talwar Consultants |
| IndiaLegal.net | TCS |
| Infocache | Technocrats Information Services |
| Information & Analytics | The Legal Outsource |
| Infosys | Thuriam BPO & Knowledge Services |
| Innovar IP Consulting Group | Total Attorneys |
| Inrea | Tricom |
| Integreon | Tusker Group |
| Intercom India | Unilaw |
| Intrust Global | UnitedLex |
| Inventurus | Variante Global |
| iRunway | Verist Research |
| Ius Juris | Williams Lea |
| JuriScout | Wipro |
| Kaizen Process Outsourcing | WiseAssist |
| Kochar LexServe | WNS |

# Appendix B

# Glossary of terms

**Bundled Services:** As one of ten LSO towers, bundled services refers to providers who offer services beyond LSO, including information technology outsourcing (ITO) and business process outsourcing (BPO) services.

**Commercial Analysis:** The assessment of risk and economic impact of alternative courses of action.

**Compliance Services:** As one of ten LSO towers, compliance services comprise research, analysis, advice, legal management, and/ or document management services to ensure compliance with regulations and policies.

**Consulting Services:** As one of the ten LSO service towers, consulting services comprise high-level strategic advice, such as helping to transform the in-house legal department or designing legal policies, processes, and solutions.

**Corporate Services:** As one of the ten LSO service towers, corporate services comprise research, document drafting, legal analysis, advice, document management, and/or legal management services to support mergers, acquisitions, transaction agreements, or corporate financing.

**Document Management:** the storing, indexing, retrieving, and sharing of physical and/or electronic documents.

**Drafting:** the creation of binding legal text, including enacted law like statutes, rules, and regulations; contracts (private and public); personal legal documents like wills and trusts; and public legal documents like notices and instructions. (Source: Wikipedia).

**Employment Services:** As one of the ten LSO service towers, employment services comprise research, document drafting, commercial analysis, legal analysis, legal action, advice, document management, and/or legal management services for employment contracts, disputes, immigration or injury.

**Intellectual Property Services:** As one of the ten LSO service towers, intellectual property services comprise research, commercial analysis, legal analysis, legal action, and/or document management services for patents, trademarks, domain names or other intellectual property.

**Legal Action:** 'The action taken by a person or legal entity against another person, persons or entities with an intention to avail legal repercussions or remedies for any loss occurred or may occur, by moving a lawsuit in the court of the land.' (Source: www.legal-explanations.com).

**Legal Advice:** In the common law, legal advice is the giving of a formal opinion regarding the substance or procedure of the law by an officer of the court, such as a solicitor or barrister. The UK's Legal Services Act 2007 includes the giving of legal advice within the definition of 'unreserved legal activities', which means that it can be provided by any person not just an officer of the court. (Source: Wikipedia)

**Legal Analysis:** The examination of legal issues and questions of law, the determination of rules or laws which govern legal issues/questions, the assessment of how the law applies to the legal issues/questions, and the conclusion or summarisation of results. (Source: www.essortment.com)

**Legal Management:** The management of resources and processes associated with a legal service.

**Litigation Services**: As one of the ten LSO service towers, litigation services comprise research, discovery, legal analysis, document management, and/or case management services associated with legal actions.

**Non-legal Services:** services that are not directly associated with a legal matter but support legal departments, such as training and office management.

**Prepare Matters:** The preparation of legal documents that form part of the legal process; 'A matter of record is the documented proceeding in a law suit consisting of recordings by the court clerk, testimony, evidence, arguments, and rulings connected with the suit.' (Source: www.legal-explanations.com).

**Property Services:** As one of the ten LSO service towers, property services comprise research, document drafting, legal analysis, legal action, advice, document management, and legal management services for purchase, lease, rent, or sale of physical property.

**Research:** The process of identifying and retrieving information necessary to support legal decision-making and includes finding primary sources of law or authority in a given jurisdiction, searching secondary sources such as law reviews, legal dictionaries, legal treatises, and legal encyclopedias, or searching non-legal sources. (Source: Wikipedia)

**Resourcing:** As one of the ten LSO service towers, resourcing comprises staff augmentation of administrators, paralegals, or lawyers.

**Services Procurement:** As one of the ten LSO service towers, services procurement comprises research, document drafting, commercial analysis, legal analysis, advice, document management, and/or legal management services for contracts, service agreements, or outsourcing.

# Index

account leadership, 36
acquisitions, 182–3
Actis, 182
Affiliated Computer Services
    (ACS), 182
Alpha-Client, 46–7
Alpha-Provider, 47
Alternative Business Structure
    (ABS), 102, 181–2
alternative journeys, 91–7
analytics, 164–6
attitude
collaborative, 154–5
relational governance, 72
automation software, 185
Axiom, 118–22

behaviour
    collaborative, 155–7
    management, 37
    in relational governance, 72
bellweather deals, 3–4
Beta-Client, 47–8
Beta-Provider, 47–8
blue chip work, 179
Brown, Liam, 122–7
BT, 3
bundled services, 21, 176–7
Burgess, Andrew, 2–3
business management capability,
    36–7

business outcomes, 161–4
Business Process Outsourcing
    (BPO), 3
    bundled services, 177
    collaborative governance, 153–7
    concerns with, 174
    locations, 183–4
    mergers and acquisitions, 182
business re-engineering, 38

Cameron McKenna, 3
captive centre, moving from a,
    46–7
Carillion, 114–18
challenges, 8–12, 81
change management, 157–60,
    167–8
changing market, 80
China, 26
Cinven Partners, 183
client capabilities, 14–15
client perspectives, 43–78
    case studies synopses, 44–51
    contractual governance, 56–61
    location of LSO staff, 75–7
    LSO relationships, 44–51
    LSO strategy, 51–5
    provider selection, 55–6
    provider turnover, 70–1
    relational governance, 72–5
    stakeholder buy-in, 61–4

transition and co-ordination of
work, 64–70
collaborative attitudes, 154–5
collaborative behaviours, 155–7
collaborative BPO governance,
153–7
communication, 68
competition, spurring, 7–8
compliance services, 20
Computer Patent Annuities
(CPA), 4
conflict resolution, 73–5
consensus management
limitations, 9
consulting services, 21
contract attribution, 93
contracting capability, 36
contractual governance, 56–61
Cooper, Leah, 3
co-ordination of work, 64–70
corporate services, 20
costs
predictability, 57–8
reduction, 11, 47–8, 49–50,
53–5, 160–1
savings, 5
CPA Global, 183
Crownbridge Group LLC, 182–3
CSC, 109–13
customer development, 40

daily rates, 23–4
data
analysis, 164–6
lack of, 11–12
Datum Legal, 182
delivery centres, 75–7

delivery competency, 33, 35
delivery speed, 6
Dell, 182
Delta-Client, 49–50
Delta-Provider, 50
diamonds, 175–6
digital assembly line, 52–3
Direct Channel Holdings, 183
disaggregating legal work, 52–3
document review, 6, 49–50, 50,
93, 184
domain expertise, 38, 164–6
domain understanding, 15
drivers of change, 94

ecosystem, legal, 97–102
eco-systems, 80–1
eDiscovery, 6, 10, 50, 91, 93,
184
eDiscovery requirements, 10
Electronic Data Systems (EDS),
182
Elevate Services, 122–7
employees, providers' *see* staff,
providers'
employment services, 20
end-to-end approach, 150–3
engagement models, 180–2
enterprise legal functions, 175–6
enterprise partnership, 180–1
Epsilon-Client, 50–1
Epsilon-Provider, 51
Europe, 26
evolutionary approach, 91–7
evolution of LSO model, 79–82
Exigent, 127–31
experience, lack of, 11–12

external benchmarking, 147–73
  business outcomes, 161–4
  change management as priority,
      157–60
  collaborative BPO governance,
      153–7
  domain expertise and analytics,
      164–6
  end-to-end approach, 150–3
  high performance definition,
      148
  relationship characteristics,
      149–50
  retained organisation
      transformation, 167–9
  technology as business enabler,
      169–71
  value beyond cost, 160–1

face-to-face meetings, 64
fees, 23–4
fixed-fee FTE pricing, 57–8
Full Time Equivalents (FTEs), 56,
      57–8

gainsharing, 60–1, 163–4
Gamma-Client, 48–9
Gamma-Provider, 48–9
Global Financial Crisis (GFC), 47
global market, 1–2, 75–7,
      183–4
Gogel, Bob, 132–6
governance, 39
  collaborative BPO, 153–7
  contractual, 56–61
  relational, 72–5
growth rate, 1–2

Hamilton, Alex, 141–4
Harris, Mark, 118–22
H3 Consulting, 183
Hewlett-Packard (HP), 182
high-level point person, 65, 159
high performance businesses see
      external benchmarking
high performance definition,
      148
high risk approach, 93
Holme, David, 127–31
hub model, 99–102
Hudson, Kathy, 3
human resource management
      capability, 15

IDS Legal, 183
India, 183
  captive centre, 46
  cost savings, 5
  market, 2
  staff turnover, 26–7
Information Technology
      Infrastructure Library
      (ITIL), 9
Information Technology
      Outsourcing (ITO), 3
  bundled services, 177
  concerns with, 174
  locations, 183–4
  mergers and acquisitions, 182
in-house lawyers, 6
  focusing on strategic work, 54
  incentives for, 63–4
  involving, 62–3
  nurturing LSO providers
      lawyers, 68

in-house staff, refocusing, 47–8
innovation agenda, 60–1
input-based pricing, 60
Integreon, 3, 5, 132–6, 182
intellectual property services, 20
IP Management software, 184
issue resolution, 73–5

jurisdictional requirements, 9

Key Performance Indicators, 63–4,
  161
Kodak, 3

law firms response, 177–8
LawScribe, 182
learning curve, 12–15
learning from other outsourced
  services, 69–70
legal panels, 48–9
legal process framework,
  83–90
  horizontal slice approach, 86,
  89–90
  managed legal service, 85, 86–7
  vertical slice approach, 85,
  88–9
Legal Services Act 2007, 181–2
Legal Services Outsourcing (LSO)
  definition, 1
legal services transformation, 52
legal service towers, 20–3
legal sourcing model, 79–82
litigation services, 20
London School of Economics and
  Political Science, 2–3
low risk approach, 91

managed legal service, 85, 86–7
management, change, 157–60
management of transformation
  programmes, 95
market development/maturing,
  11
market predictions, 174–87
  bundled services, 176–7
  engagement models, 180–2
  law firms response, 177–8
  locations, 183–4
  mergers, acquisitions and
  strategic alliances, 182–3
  panel reviews, 176–7
  shape-shift of enterprise legal
  functions, 175–6
  technology, 184–5
Master Service Agreement (MSA),
  57
Matter Management software,
  184
mergers, 182–3
Microsoft, 3–4
multi-shore model, 76

Nienaber, Gawie, 109–13

objectives, 93–4
offshore models, 10
offshore resources, 27, 28
Onshore Engagement Manager
  (OEM), 65–6
onshore resources, 27, 28
ONSIGHT3, 182
opponents to LSO, 62
optimisation, 95
organisational design, 40

organisational drivers for change, 94
output-based pricing, 59

panel reviews, 176–7
panels, legal, 48–9
pangea3, 182
partnership attitude, 154–7
Partnership View, 72–3
people management, 37
performance, 149
Perot Systems, 182
Philippines, 2, 5, 183
pilot projects, 12
planning capability, 36
playbooks, 66–7, 71
portals, 67
pricing, 23–4, 56–7
  fixed-fee FTE, 57–8
  unit, 58–9
  utility, 6–7
process maturity, lack of, 9
productivity improvements, yearly, 60
programme management, 39
progress measurement, 160
property services, 20
provider market structure, 10
provider(s)
  capabilities, 15, 55–6
  capabilities model, 32–41
  clients selection of, 55–6
  competencies, 29–32, 33–5
  geographic reach, 27
  landscape, 2, 19–42
  legal service towers, 20–3
  location, 75–7, 183–4
pricing, 23–4
revenues, 24
size: headcount, 25–7
skill sets, 21–2
small base of, 11
team composition, 27–9
testing capabilities, 56
treating as partners, 72–3
turnover, 70–1
value chain rise, 178–9
proving the concept of LSO, 63
*Provocations and Perspectives,* 6
pyramids, 175–6

qualification requirements, 9
quality of work, 7, 50–1
  improving, 54

radiant.law, 141–4
rates, 23–4
red chip work, 178–9
Reed, Dan, 137–41
re-engineering processes, 81–2
relational governance, 72–5
relationship competency, 34, 35
research, 2–3
resolution of conflicts/issues, 73–5
resource-based pricing, 59
resourcing, 20
retained organisation
  transformation, 167–9
Rio Tinto, 3
risk averseness, 8

Satyam, 183
scalability, 6, 49–50, 54
service issues, 73–5

Service Level Agreements (SLAs),
56–7
services procurement, 20
service towers, 20–3
shape-shift of enterprise legal
functions, 175–6
sizing a market, 1–2
skill sets, 21–2
Sommer, Christian, 106–9
sourcing expertise, 38–9, 95
sourcing process, 82
staff, providers', 25–7
management, 37
turnover, 26–7
stakeholder buy-in, 61–4
standardised work, 58–9, 95
statements of Work (SOW), 57
strategic alliances, 182–3
strategy, 51–5
supplier management capability, 14
Susskind, Richard, 6

tactical projects, 10
Tapp, Richard, 114–18
targets, staying on, 160
technical and methodological
capability, 14, 15
technology
as business enabler, 169–71
exploitation, 38
market predictions, 184–5
specialist, 11

test cases, 3–4
Thomson Reuters', 182
tipping point of LSO market,
79–80
transaction-based pricing, 59
transformational leaders, 159
transformation competency, 34,
35
transformation programme, 94–7,
164, 167–9
transition of work, 64–70
triage function, 99

UnitedLex, 3, 137–41, 182–3
unit pricing, 58–9
US market, 1–2
eDiscovery requirements, 10
staff turnover, 26
utility pricing, 6–7

value addition, 54–5
value chain, 178–9
value proposition, 4–8
Vodafone, 106–9
volume of work, 58–9

white chip work, 178
Wipro, 4
work transition and co-ordination,
64–70

Xerox, 182